THE BLACK BRIDGE

THE BLACK BRIDGE

One Man's War With Himself

MICHAEL TANNER

authorHOUSE®

AuthorHouse™
1663 Liberty Drive
Bloomington, IN 47403
www.authorhouse.com
Phone: 1-800-839-8640

Published by AuthorHouse   10/29/2012

ISBN: 978-1-4772-3909-4 (sc)
ISBN: 978-1-4772-3908-7 (hc)
ISBN: 978-1-4772-3910-0 (e)

Contents

WHICH OF US IS NOT FOREVER A STRANGER AND ALONE?

Thomas Wolfe

I HAVE NOT LOVED THE WORLD, NOR THE WORLD ME
Lord Byron

He examined the bird closely. Strange, he mused, how the oddest thing can fascinate a man when confronted by eternity.

Listening to the birds serenading the dawn, and resting his hands on his knees, he knew he would not feel afraid. He attributed this to fear being no more of an irritant to him now than hunger or thirst. He had gone through it in his imagination and it had turned out fine. He was unafraid now.

Instead, he concentrated on the birds. He watched one glide to earth near his feet and smiled. The robin reminded him of freedom, of hope: of home, of Oxford, of bursting out onto the pitch at the Iffley Road rugby ground, of tubbing on a glassy Isis of a sunlit afternoon; and of Christmas when the selfsame red rascal would peer from the ranks of Christmas-card snowman and reindeers, when even he had found occasion to enjoy the company of his fellow man. Apart, that is, from the one just passed.

Such a quintessentially English bird, the officer decided: resourceful; bursting with energy; chirpy; indefatigable. As English as . . . he ransacked his brain for a simile that pleased . . . plum loaf! His lips pursed at the sheer eccentricity of his choice. Yes, plum loaf! Then the crinkles faded. How could one of England's own be at home in this cheerless corner of northern France?

His brown eyes followed the robin's progress to the exclusion of all else going on around him. The germ of a second smile briefly troubled the cracked corners of his mouth as he studied the bird excavating the gravel

1

around his feet for grubs until it finally cocked its head in beak-filled triumph and fixed him with a challenging stare of its own. The officer stuck out his tongue.

It was a mizzly April dawn, the air heavy with a hammam's dampness that made him set his jaw lest anyone interpret a shiver as a sign of failing courage. He adjusted his seat, planted his feet firmly in the gravel until it scrunched and pressed his backbone hard against the centre rail of the simple wooden chair until he felt spine and timber as one. Then, aping his avian companion, he puffed out his chest and lifted his chin. Running a finger along the envelope pressed against his right knee, he closed his eyes.

He pictured himself on a rusting iron bridge, a spindly 13-year-old with tangled hair clad in nothing but a pair of baggy long-johns, his wet toes teetering on the slippery rim of the central arch, cold terror paralyzing his limbs. He recalled gulping air into his lungs until they seemed to ram themselves against his ribcage, and how he'd stared repeatedly at the inky waters of the Thames eddying some 20 feet below. Hanging from the girders of the bridge were his peers; some egging him on but most of them jeering at his reluctance to launch himself into the unknown. Now, on this morning, he knew dozens of other eyes would be scrutinizing him just as keenly.

Even though he could not see them. All he saw was a carefree girl in a thin cotton dress looking radiant on a golden July evening, auburn tresses stroking her shoulders, her freckled face lit by a generous smile he hoped he had helped place there. And for the second time in his short life he blew her a kiss farewell.

Shards of watery sunlight danced off the buttons of his tunic as it rose and fell in measured, contented rhythm, his breath coming more steadily now, conveying serenity to every part of his body. He re-set his palms, cool and free of sweat, on his thighs, spread his fingers and thought he saw his brother waiting to greet him. He promised they would soon sleep together in eternity.

The young man was at peace with himself, resigned to dying in his own arms having lived in similar isolation. He was happy to shake hands with death. He felt no urge to rage against the dying of the light for he welcomed the longest and darkest night, shedding no tear at deserting a world from which he felt alienated.

After permitting himself one final glance at the robin's scarlet vest, he cleared his mind, blew out his cheeks and closed his eyes on life.

At last there was a bullet with his number on it and he was glad.

1

Holnon Wood

'Lanham, I've a job for you. It will, in my honest opinion, suit you admirably.'

Captain John Adamson thrust a sheet of paper toward the young subaltern stood at attention in front of the upturned tea-chest that doubled as his desk without raising his eyes from a second sheet that he was in the process of signing. He didn't like the man and saw no reason to disguise the fact.

Max Lanham accepted the paper from his spaniel-jowled company commander and scanned its contents. He got as far as 'The following detail from the 2/4th Battalion Oxford & Bucks Light Infantry will be sent to Caulaincourt Chateau tonight, returning to Holnon Wood on completion of the duty. Transport is to be arranged for . . . 'without hesitation but then felt the need to steady himself.

His eyes narrowed until concentration had almost consumed them but the final sentences remained as chilling as a January night in no-man's-land: 'Firing Party—one officer, one NCO and nine men. On arrival at Caulaincourt this party should be confined to the billets which will be allotted to them by the 1st Battalion Royal Warwickshire Regiment. The men need not be informed of the duty for which they have been detailed until the morning of the 9th May inst.'

'A distasteful job, I'm afraid,' added Adamson, continuing to wade through his pile of paperwork with the detached air of a former Oxford don who wished himself back in the Bodleian Library. He rubbed index fingers against the sides of his nose, causing the purple veins to stand out even more vividly. 'But someone has got to do it.'

He smirked. 'The Warwicks don't want to do it themselves, so I've given it to 16 platoon. See that it's completed properly.'

Adamson pushed his papers aside and finally consented to look up. He did not see one of his youngest, ablest and most battle-hardened officers; failed to register the sallow cheeks of fatigue nor eyes weary at what they had been forced to witness. The men under his command were little more than statistics to him nowadays: numbers on parade; numbers in sick bay; numbers dead and missing. All he registered was a cipher with no more distinguishing features than those fitting the standard police description of 'medium height; medium build; brown hair; brown eyes.'

Lanham would not have taken issue. He considered his appearance utterly nondescript. He felt his nose was too pudgy, his jaw line too weak, his lips too thick and his eyes, well, although he liked to believe their shade of brown hinted at ochre, he reluctantly conceded they more than merited their school label of 'piss-holes in the snow.'

His one physical attribute, admired by female acquaintances of a certain age, was a fine head of hair which rose from his forehead in a thick wave and paid homage to the long cavalier ringlets of infancy captured in a photograph hanging in the dining room back home. His natural expression, though lively and alert, seldom showed itself: he had the power of making his face look dull and so disinterested that people either failed to notice him or concluded he was too aloof to bother with. He had entertained notions of adding a moustache to lend character but once he saw the laughable efforts of other subalterns he quickly abandoned any such idea. He hoped that character might come with age.

'By the book, Lanham,' sighed Adamson. 'None of your highly personal and exceedingly lax interpretation of Army Regulations. The Army is no place for loose cannons.'

He stifled a smile at his play on words and manufactured a glare instead. 'And a haircut wouldn't come amiss either.'

The lieutenant folded the orders and put them in his breast pocket. He snapped off a salute and left the dilapidated greenhouse pressed into service as D company's HQ without complaint. But his mind was rewinding the blazing argument he'd had with Adamson on returning from the Fayet raid. Bawling out one's CO was the act of an idiot, he told himself, which was bound to have repercussions.

Once outside he removed his hat and clapped his forehead lest his rage spewed forth. His lips began quivering. It was bad enough being a dogsbody, he thought to himself, but he might at least be one to a decent dog. 'You petty, mean-spirited bastard!'

Lanham trudged back to his platoon, currently resting-up in a sandy railway cutting where it had been enjoying the rare bliss of some decent food from proper cookers and some decent sleep secure from shelling, and ordered his sergeant to select one corporal and nine men for a special detail.

Within the hour Sergeant Clinkard had the men assembled behind their transport. Lanham stood beside the nearby stump of a decapitated railway signal, tapping his gloved fingers on the splintered timber, wondering how he would cope with the ensuing 24 hours. The dirt-filled lines on his forehead darkened as he swept a hand through his mop of wavy chestnut hair.

He kicked the base of the stump: almost 12 months in the trenches and his decision to volunteer remained as inexplicable as it did at the time. Had patriotism, that 'last refuge of a scoundrel,' been his undoing when his school received a visit from a be-medalled recruiting sergeant on the eve of war? No: causes meant more to him than any blind loyalty to his country. Putting his manhood to the extreme test? He'd never drawn a white feather but, though he hated to admit it, quite possibly. He couldn't escape the conclusion that it all came down to teenage impetuosity, nothing more than a rush of blood. Enlisting was an act of sheer folly; yet foolishness was not a trait he'd ever recognized in himself.

Fighting for the sake of fighting was anathema to him. Athletically inclined though he became by the time he left school, his sport of choice was rugby football where physical violence, he argued, was not an end in itself. Resisting the primal urges of the boxing ring, his school's most prestigious sporting arena, came easily. He never considered himself to be a 'fighter' of any description: pillow fights, ragging and dorm raids saw him a disinterested spectator. As for any commitment to the Combined Cadet Force, his sloppiness on parade declared an indifference verging on insubordination.

And yet here he was: 12 months under fire. Most subalterns lasted six weeks. Doing his family and country proud. And not a medal or even a kitten scratch to show for it; no red badge of courage, the fresh scar on his forehead feeding thin violet tributaries down either side of his nose merely testament to an impromptu game of inter platoon rugby while the company had been resting-up at Atilly a fortnight ago. Twelve months doing his duty: no heroics but no backsliding either. Yet here he was, still just a lieutenant. Still first in line for the shit jobs. A shit job like this one.

He suspected his men knew they had drawn the shit-job of all shit-jobs. Ten men—including 16 platoon's best sharpshooters—for a special detail at another battalion's headquarters to the rear of the front line: it was obvious what was going on. It was now common knowledge among all ranks that the Commander-in-Chief's pledge 'to maintain the highest standard of discipline' had resulted in 'the infliction of the most severe punishment' on at least 150 occasions along the Western Front by the spring of 1917. And a firing party was invariably brought in from outside because a battalion never wanted to be seen shooting one of its own.

Lanham switched his attention to his men, smoking a last pipe or cigarette before climbing aboard the lorry: hunched shoulders and the odd furtive glance in his direction needed no translation. At this moment he knew every man-jack of them loathed him. One emerged from the bunch and advanced toward him with the conviction of a German offensive. Lanham knew who it would be even as he heard the footsteps and before he raised his eyes.

'Sir, p'mission to speak!'

'What is it, Bostock?'

'I wants a word with you, man-to-man like?' said Hector Bostock, his vowels elongated in the manner of every 'Orks-ferd' voice in the platoon by pronouncing such as 'wants' as 'waunts' and 'like' as 'loik.'

Bostock leered in the general direction of his mates, a slyness exacerbated by his eyes having the odd habit of moving fractionally slower than his head. He tipped back his helmet, revealing a close-cropped ginger hairline, rubbed his nose and made to speak. 'Summut the men waunts me to say . . .'

'Sar'nt Clinkard!' Lanham shouted, halting Bostock as if he'd been slapped with a sprung sapling. 'Get the men aboard the transport.'

The 20-year veteran of Omdurman and Mafeking largely responsible for teaching Lanham everything he knew about leading men in battle instantly shrieked in the positive. The men groaned, and then obeyed, their hopes of sport dashed.

'Well, Bostock, what is it?' their officer said in a stage whisper. He could feel his heart thumping against his tunic.

'We don't loik it,' Bostock replied, just as conspiratorially. 'We reck'n we know what this detail's up for an' one a two o' the men are worried about it.'

'Captain Adamson has seen fit to take you into his confidence then?'

Bostock spread himself like a cobra's hood. He was the son of a blacksmith and shared the forge with his father like a pair of land-locked Vikings, proud of the physique genes and trade had combined to create. A ruddy complexion, varying in shades of redness as if it had been the victim of rough handling with a scrubbing brush, was heightened by a proclivity for free sweating. His slab of a forehead was as deep as it was wide, overhanging his eyes in the manner of a cliff face protecting a couple of menacing caves. A uniform that made no concession to matching a lean trunk to spectacularly muscular limbs merely made him appear more intimidating.

He leant on his rifle with the cockiness he considered irresistible to the village girls of Littlemore. 'No, not 'xactly . . .'

He edged forward, the eyes and mouth that had been working in insolent tandem hardening into tramlines of anger.

'It's plain as the nose on your face what we're up to,' he hissed. 'Some poor bleeder's for the high jump an' we're givin' 'im the push.'

Lanham waited for the pay-off line. With Bostock there was always a pay-off line for he was a nourisher of mischief.

'They en't got no stomach for it,' Bostock said, now almost nose to nose with his superior. 'They'd loik to be 'xcused duty. They don't waunter do it.'

Lanham felt a hot choking temper rise in his throat and looked away to compose himself. Every atom of his being commanded he snatch Bostock's rifle and smash the stock under his jaw until those insolent lips stopped moving. That is, every atom except those reminding him such actions were not only beneath an officer but also guaranteed to see him court-martialled and cashiered in disgrace.

'Sam, cop what 'Ector just said to the lef-tenant?'

Private Arthur Goodey was lip-reading the conversation thanks to a convenient tear in the lorry's canvas. 'He'll be on a fizzer for that!'

Sam Dewe took the cigarette from his mouth and cupped it in his right hand behind his back. 'Ector knows how to get right up Boy Wonder's nose a'right. Here, shove over, let me have a gander. If you ask me, Eck's got him on the run.'

'He shouldner speak to the lef-tenant like that,' continued Goodey. 'He looked out for us at Fayet, didn't he? Put 'is head on the block an' all. Told Cap'n Adamson we shouldner gone. He's a decent chap.'

Goodey glanced around for support. Nobody seemed to be listening.

'I wouldn't let our 'Ector hear you sayin' that if I wuz you.'

'I'll tell him straight to his face!'

Dewe's flat farmer's face imploded with a lopsided grin. 'Yes! An' that bum fluff on your chin's a beard I s'pose!'

The rest joined in the gurning. Goodey weighed barely seven stone wringing wet and only just exceeded the Army minimum height—and then only after it had been reduced to five feet and he'd brushed his blond hair so it stuck up like frosted straw on a stone. His pinched face and dancer's body seemed suggestive of the stage, but his father wanted him to be a jockey like Steve Donoghue and got him apprenticed to Charles Morton at Letcombe Regis. The first morning Goodey was legged up on the stable hack he slid off the other side and ran away to hide in the tack room. When his fellow apprentices found him they showed their compassion, as young apprentices will, by burying him up to his neck in the muck heap. Goodey returned to Littlemore after two days.

Put a set of reins in his hands and Goodey proved inarticulate. It was his misfortune to be articulate with a gun. He was the son of a gamekeeper and could plug the eye of a rabbit at a hundred yards with a rifle. Like Bostock he was a conscript—unlike Dewe who had volunteered in 1915—but as a qualified marksman he earned an extra sixpence a day.

'We're lucky havin' an officer like Lef-tenant Lanham,' he squeaked from behind his palm. 'An' thass gospel!'

Goodey's soft-boiled eyes once more sought allies while his fingers searched his chin for invisible bristles. No one paid him heed. Everyone else was straining to catch events a dozen yards away.

They saw Bostock keep his officer waiting for as long as he dared before condescending to execute a slack-wristed salute, and then greeted with rising mirth the sight of Lanham's facial muscles jumping as molar ground against molar.

'As usual, Bostock, you're slicker than snot on a doorknob,' they heard him say, his voice all of a tremor. 'You'd not recognize duty unless it wore a skirt. Now, get into the lorry along with the others. You'll do as you're told, and you'll do your damn duty!'

'Know me place, issit?'

'You—we—are not back home now!' Lanham's upper body shook.

'But one day we will, one day this bloomin' war'll be over,' sneered Bostock. 'Then we'll see who's top dog.'

'Here, your word carries no weight. Here, you'll do as I say! I am top dog here and don't you forget it!'

Bostock grinned and began patting his crotch. 'Just time to strain me spuds, sir, 'fore we go?'

Without waiting for an answer he ambled behind a nearby hedgerow. After a leisurely pee he casually vaulted into the back of the lorry. He elbowed Goodey aside to park himself next to Dewe and immediately dug his hand into Dewe's breast pocket, extricating a crumpled cigarette which he waited to be lit for him.

'Not me Woodbine!' cried Dewe. 'Been savin' that. Have one o' these Trumpeters.'

'Not smokin' that horse shit,' countered Bostock, blowing a column of blue smoke against the canvas above his head before picking a fleck of tobacco off his tongue and executing another cheek-dimpling drag.

'No balls!' he grunted and looked around for approval: his glare was met by a shrug or a nod of assent. 'Ask Zena Boas!'

Dewe puffed out his cheeks. His industrial eyebrows arched, and the leathery skin charged with retaining the flesh of his face, stretched to capacity at the best of times, now gave him the expression of a gurnard flexing its gills. He got as far as saying 'Loik to do more than ask . . . 'before his words were drowned by a chorus of 'Whorr!'

'Never did have any balls!' continued Bostock. 'Not as a kid! Not on Black Bridge. Not now! Never will!'

'Thass never right . . .'

'Shut up, Goodey, you moron!' cut in Bostock.

He sniffed and took another drag. 'Hear about Goodey's Christmas present from his ma? Two-piece jigsaw puzzle, it were. He gave it away. Couldn't do it. Said there wuz no picture on the box!'

The lorry rocked on its axles along to the guffaws.

'Corp'l Fenn!' bellowed Clinkard. 'It sounds like the tap-room of The George on a Saturday night back there—keep those men quiet! This is not a bloody picnic they're going on!'

The two rows of tin hats facing each other in the back of the lorry tipped forward to muffle the sniggering that began to accompany the pop-pop-pop of the lorry's motor.

'Sar'nt!' Lanham called out. 'Make it absolutely clear to every man on this detail that if anyone utters so much as one more word of dissention he'll find himself on a charge. Have I made myself fully understood?'

Clinkard marched to the rear of the lorry and thrust his head between the canvas flaps. 'I do hope you all heard the lieutenant and paid attention! Some of you, Bostock, more than bleedin' others.'

Clinkard's glare wiped the scowl from Bostock's face as comprehensively as a blackboard duster.

'Keep a close eye on them, Mister Lanham!' said the sergeant on returning to his officer's side.

He paused for a moment, as if expecting a response. 'Remember, sir, what I told you in camp. You are not the friend from home any more. Don't give them bastards an inch.'

'Thank you sar'nt, as ever, for the advice,' Lanham said, picking up his white Burberry trench coat. 'You may be sure that I won't.'

'Sir,' the sergeant said more anxiously, 'don't forget what I always say about those coats . . .'

'Yes, I know! Sniper's dream!'

At last he registered the concern on Clinkard's face. 'I'll be careful where I wear it.'

'Right you are, sir.'

With that Lanham walked toward the truck, an old refrain thrumming round and round his brain: 'What is a 22-year-old been-nowhere and done-nothing doing here in charge of an execution squad?'

Then he remembered.

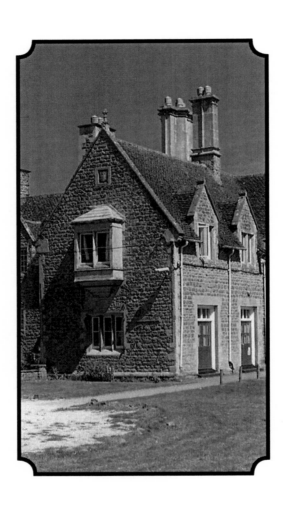

2

Lawn Upton

He'd been relaxing in the library at Lawn Upton, his family home in the village of Littlemore, just outside Oxford on the road to Henley.

The library was the one place he felt liberated, freed by the books covering every inch of wall space from floor to ceiling apart from that occupied by the Charles Napier Hemy seascape depicting a vessel in distress on the Goodwin Sands which hung over the fireplace. The collection was the legacy of his grandfather Herbert Lanham, who, to his despair, failed to pass on his bibliophile tendencies to his only son. Max calculated that there must be around 2000 volumes on the walnut shelves: he reckoned he'd read barely a hundred of them but he knew for a fact his father seldom bothered to open even one. The only books Roy Lanham read were *Racing Up-To-Date* and *Ruffs Guide to the Turf*, neither of which were permitted in the house let alone the library—they were left in Len Goodey's care down at the lodge.

Max loved the world books enabled him to access at the turn of a page. No book of his was ever thrown away; no word, however mundane, deserved to be left unread. But even more than their words, he loved their appearance, their feel. The touch of smooth morocco leather and heavy quality paper transmitted a feeling positively sensual; the vivid reds, greens and browns of glossy leather boards, their marbled endpapers and the gilt lettering of their titles he found a visual banquet. Yet the transcendent quality was their smell: in particular—even though the musty pong of mildewed paper was not unattractive to Max—it was the aroma of leather. The world of books reeked of leather, just like the explosion of leather that hit Max's nostrils when he opened the box on a brand new pair of rugby boots from Elmer Cotton's sports-shop in The Turl. Max would spend as many hours polishing his leather-bound copies of *Our Island Story*, *Treasure Island* and *Beau Geste*—in the process checking that every page had not been dog-eared or accidentally bent out of shape—as he would his favourite boots. In Max's ideal world he would play rugby twice a week and earn his living as an archivist in the Bodleian: the former was within his grasp but since 'The Bod' only recruited one trainee archivist every ten years or so he deemed his chances of managing the latter decidedly slim.

Once he had finally selected and eased the afternoon's reading from its shelf and slumped into his battered Charles Bevan leather reclining armchair in the corner, splaying his legs over the arm in the way his mother found so uncouth, no interruption of any kind would be tolerated.

Especially it were *that* voice. The voice, deep, dark and commanding, that reminded him why school holidays were more of a trial than school terms and why his stomach presently felt as if he had overindulged himself with marshmallow.

'Max, Mr Tinegate is here to see you.'

'Not that insufferable prig!'

'Max! How dare you use that language to your mother!'

Reluctantly Max put down his book and slowly gave Naomi Lanham his full attention.

Only just into her forties, she could have passed for ten years younger. Eyes capable of changing from grey to ebony with her mood, precipitous cheekbones and a wide mouth framed by generous lips set against a flawless complexion generated a mesmeric beauty that had endeared her to members of Oxford's artist fraternity prior to her marriage. So had her body, for it was the full-bosomed and narrow-hipped model beloved by Titian.

'Mr Tinegate has made time in his busy schedule to see you . . .'

'Why?'

'Because I asked him to.'

Every single vowel extended, every consonant cutting, she fluttered her eyelashes and flicked her nut-brown hair in the manner of a freshening breeze heralding a tempest.

'Oh, so that's all right then!'

'You really can be quite tiresome! Mr Tinegate has come with an offer . . .'

'An offer? What can he offer me? He runs a piddling sawmill over the road . . .'

'Language!'

Her son picked up his book again and started flicking through the pages aimlessly. He was already imagining what she might say next so that he could counter with some suitably acerbic riposte.

'As you know, Mr Tinegate has no son and he would like to appoint you deputy manager of the mill with a view to assuming control one day. Isn't that kind of him?'

Max lobbed the book back onto the table and rocked with theatrical laughter. 'Wherever did he get a silly idea like that?'

A moment's thought supplied the answer. 'Oh, of course, you put the idea in his head.'

Naomi Lanham's reply was delayed by the sudden appearance of her husband—though speed of movement was a characteristic she no longer associated with him. He looked toward his wife of 25 years like a novitiate asking his abbot for permission to break a vow of silence. When no rebuke seemed forthcoming, he spoke: 'Did you know that Mr Tinegate is waiting in the drawing room, dear?'

'Hello, Royal!' Max said jauntily, quick to scent an opportunity to cause embarrassment.

'Don't call your father by that silly name! You know he detests it! Roy is quite sufficient.'

It was true that Royal Lanham had never been comfortable with his christened name and he looked suitably chastened on this occasion also. He looked that much older than his true age as his wife looked younger than hers. As the photograph on a side table testified, twenty years ago he had cut a roguishly handsome figure. But nowadays his brushed-back, brilliantine slicked, dark brown centre-parted hair was thinning and fading to silver about the temples and the lines that ran from his fleshy nostrils to his rounded chin looked as if they had been cut by rainwater. Moreover, it appeared as if someone had recently severed his facial muscles, causing every feature to sag like those of an ageing bloodhound. If this leathery, hangdog facade was not the outward sign of a sad, broken-spirited man, it certainly suggested as much to his son.

'Yes I did,' his wife continued, looking as if she'd just sucked on a lemon. 'Max and I are discussing something vital. Arrange for some tea to be sent in, and then Mr Tinegate may join us.'

'Right you are then!'

Max watched his father sidle toward the door, head bowed and cocked to one side, with a silly servile grin on his face that Max longed to knock off: if only, wished Max, he would launch a counter-attack occasionally instead of taking headlong flight. This was his house. Lawn Upton was his family legacy. Max hated seeing him behave like a flunkey?

'Look, mother,' he said. 'I've not done all this extra work at school to win a place at Oxford only to give it up in favour of a tin-pot position in a sawmill!'

'Max, you must look at the bigger picture . . .'

'What do you mean? Rembrandt's Night Watch? Ceiling of the Sistine Chapel? . . .'

'Oh, do act your age! I'd hoped that juvenile facetiousness was just a passing phase!'

Max returned his mother's glare. 'Bigger picture? What kind of tosh is that?'

'Mr Tinegate has . . . connections!'

'Connections?'

'Political connections,' his mother replied with a hint of conspiracy in her voice. 'He's secretary of the local branch of the Conservative party and is prepared to give you a leg-up. The Tory party is desperate for top-class recruits. Eager young men of vision who can build the future of this country. A seat on the council and a smooth transition to a parliamentary seat . . .'

'All mapped out for me, eh?' said Max, barely able to finish his sentence without Laughing. 'Looks good to have an MP in the family?'

His mother lifted her nose and looked away. She suspected it would come to this but, why-oh-why did it always have to be this way? Why was her son too stubborn to see what was best for him? She could: why not he?

'It's always about appearances, isn't it mother?' Max said, pulling a sour face and adopting a prissy voice. 'Look at Max's new suit . . . it cost five guineas from Reeds but doesn't he look smart! We're sending him to a new school . . . he'll be so much happier there.'

'Max, do see sense when it stares you in the face!' she railed. 'There's a war on! There'll be no college! The mill provides a reserved occupation! It's the sensible course of action! You can go to college when the war's over!'

Max stared in disbelief at the woman he once described in his diary as 'famine, flood, fire and pestilence.'

After a lifetime of feeling emotionally abandoned by his proper family, the sense of belonging that supposedly came with an army family suddenly seemed a God-send. The following day, 8 September 1914, Max filed into the front quad of Exeter College to kiss the bible and sign away his life at the flag-draped recruiting desk with the newly-raised 2/4th Battalion of the Oxford & Bucks Light Infantry instead of embarking on the undergraduate career he had striven so hard to attain.

He was nineteen years and five months old.

3

To Caulaincourt

Max climbed into the front seat of the truck and informed the driver of their destination. Then he slumped back in his seat and closed his eyes, his sub-conscious drifted back to the night of 27-28th April and the raid on Fayet that he was positive had seen him delegated this unenviable task.

He detested raids and that on Fayet had been as unsuccessful as it had been unnecessary. Unlike an attack, whose objective was to drive the enemy from ground he occupied and stay there, the purpose of a raid was to penetrate a portion of his front, to kill or capture as many as possible, and then retire. No attempt was made to hold the ground—which made the whole enterprise rather pointless in his opinion. Moreover, unlike attacks, raids invariably took place at night. Stumbling around in the pitch dark seemed to Max the preserve of madmen: he had never forgotten his first raid when two of his men were shot by their own comrades.

Persistent German shelling had prevented the raid from starting on time. At 3 am Max's party had still not budged from their assembly area in a sunken road on the southern edge of the village. With dawn expected shortly after 4 am, the odds of successfully negotiating the mile of no-man's-land and slipping 38 men through the narrow gap in the German line undetected began to dwindle. Lanham sent Dewe to

Adamson, requesting permission to abort the raid. Adamson ordered him to proceed.

Max's concerns seemed misplaced when the operation began promisingly. The hole in the line was duly located and numerous Germans were caught in their beds and dispatched where they lay. Unfortunately, the copses and trenches behind the front line were neither unoccupied nor so weakly defended as Intelligence had promised. Dawn broke to the chatter of murderous machine-gun fire and Max ordered a withdrawal, only for a third of his force to be scythed down re-crossing the open ground in the broad daylight. All his Littlemore boys had to show for their bravery were two captured machine-guns and one prisoner; Max was left to write letters home to the families of Wanley, Hebborn and Treadwell.

Max saw to it that his men were fed and tended before trying to walk-off his anger in the reserve trenches. But he could not. It had had plenty of time to fester, and his words ample time to form. Flinging his tin hat onto the duckboards so hard it lodged between the planks, he strode into the mess where his company commander was still at breakfast. Adamson halted in mid-chew, a blob of marmalade falling from the end of his knife, as Max's carefully worded invective filled the mess tent; he had a way with words that cut as deep as any bayonet, perfectly able, as Lt Swain attested, of persuading an angel that his harp was out of tune. Unfortunately, he was less adept at knowing when it was prudent to be economical with them, a trait viewed with suspicion by institutions like the Army.

Max was jolted back to the present by a sound like a gigantic newspaper being torn in half. Even half asleep the sound of a German 5.9 was unmistakable and he automatically ducked his head, like everyone else in the lorry. The veins of his temples bulged beneath his hands and terror soaked his spine as he visualized the shell's nose piercing skin and gristle and bone and exploding the charge that would make him feel as if he had a splitting headache all over for about a fiftieth of a second before his remains were spread over the earth and hung up in the poplar trees. He held his breath and tried to press deeper into the seat, tensing every muscle as though by sheer will power he might cheat death and defy God.

He waited until the noise changed to something resembling Joe Tutty's haywain skidding down Heyford Hill Lane with its brakes locked, a screech rising to a shriek, and then looked up just in time to see the shell bury itself about 50 yards away in a nearby field, catapulting a black fountain the size of a house high into the air and a trail of smoke coiling away on the breeze. The blast forced the air from his lungs and chafed the skin along his cheekbones. He gripped his left elbow with his other hand to minimize the shaking, an act as automatic to him lately as steadying his razor of a morning.

Then he felt a tingle of exhilaration course through him, energizing every cell and nerve in his body: the feeling he always got when the shelling stopped and he knew he was still alive. The air smelt fresher; his brain felt invigorated. It was the exquisite sensation that accompanied survival.

'Everyone all right back there?' he shouted. The only response was a symphony of sniffing and coughing. 'Corp'l Fenn! All right back there?'

Finally, there came a faint reply in the affirmative. Max examined his fingers to check they had stopped trembling. 'Keep your heads down!'

The lorry had left the comparative safety of Holnon Wood and joined the main road from St Quentin to Albert, a treacherous stretch of road pockmarked with shell holes that reduced its progress to walking pace and left its passengers dreading further salvos. The 5.9 was bad enough but what if it should be a 420 howitzer that could hurl a one-ton shell six miles at 1700 mph? They had bad dreams of taking a bayonet in the stomach. But they had nightmares about artillery. They had all seen the craters pooled with red, body parts driven into the earth, stuffed in like rags, a protruding limb sticking up as some kind of ghoulish memorial. No man wanted to be dismembered, torn to pieces, reduced to pulp, vaporized. To be wiped from the face of the earth. No body for his loved ones to bury. Not worthy of a grave.

'What about a sing-song?' said Goodey, lifting his head and straightening his helmet. '*Ink-ee Pink-ee Par-lee-voo!*'

Dewe told him where to stick his song. The soppy grin slid from Goodey's face and he returned to polishing the sight on his rifle. 'An' watch where you're pointing that bleedin' thing!'

The lorry chugged another five miles with every occupant keeping his own counsel before eventually turning off into the tranquility of the Caulaincourt sector. The chateau was familiar territory. Only a month ago it had served as their own HQ; prior to that it had played host to a German corps. It was now wrecked beyond recognition: most of its roof gone; its windows shattered. The grounds, too, were a sorry sight. Where there were once finely manicured lawns there were craters. Any trees that had survived bombardment had been cut for fuel. Even the ornamental fish ponds had been trawled for food.

A corporal was waiting to direct the men to their billet while Max was escorted to the officers mess in what remained of the chateau's *grand salon*. He was immediately drawn to one side by the regimental chaplain, to whom fell the grim task of sitting through the night with the condemned man.

The condemned soldier, Max learned, had been missing from his unit for six days when he was discovered in the docks at Boulogne.

'Might he just have gone AWOL?' asked Max. 'Got drunk on some leave . . .'

'Afraid not. They found Private . . .'

'Please, padre, I'd rather not know the man's name.'

'I understand . . . the Redcaps found him dressed in civilian clothing. Clearly trying to make a home run. Had no intention of returning to the front line. That made it a charge of desertion. A capital offence.'

'I see,' said Max. But, really, he didn't see the point at all.

The padre shifted his weight from foot to foot. 'And that's not the half of it. He had two years exemplary service to his credit, was a Kitchener volunteer back in '15.And his Field General Court Martial was held one day after he finally reached the age of 19 . . .'

'You're saying he wasn't even old enough to be on active service?' interjected Max. 'He shouldn't even have been in France?'

'That is so.'

'Good God!'

The padre's eyes widened.

'Sorry, padre, but I find this merits blasphemy.'

'Understandable, though regrettable. The subject does rouse strong emotions.'

Max didn't hear the padre's last comment. His emotions were already aroused enough. 'How old exactly is this boy? Did he enlist under-age?'

The cleric fidgeted with his dog-collar. 'The Army decrees he is the age stated on his enlistment papers—and he said he was 18.'

24

'Wasn't his age explored at the FGCM?'

'His only defence was to state that he'd "had enough of it and wanted to get out." He couldn't stand the shelling any longer.'

'So, the boy was quite clearly mentally unhinged!'

'Mental abnormality is an acceptable defence. But, unfortunately, the Army prides itself on not recruiting "the mentally abnormal." His plea was dismissed. No address in mitigation of sentence was made on his behalf and the court sentenced him to death. The sentence was confirmed by Field Marshal Haig.'

'You cannot possibly agree with this barbarity, padre?'

'My calling insists I should not but . . .'

'But?' queried Max with a shake of the head. 'There's a 'but'?'

The padre cleared his throat. 'If you will permit me to explain . . .'

Max waved a hand.

'Alas,' continued the padre in a voice barely above a whisper, 'I have to say I think the Field Marshal is right, the supreme penalty is absolutely essential. If men begin to feel they only had to walk off during a battle and then come back afterwards in order to escape death or mutilation this war would be lost in a fortnight. Examples must be made. Must be seen to be made.'

Max stared at the ceiling and loosed a lung-emptying sigh. 'You can't honestly believe justice has been done in this case?'

'I'll leave that to Almighty God to decide.'

Max harrumphed loudly enough to attract the attention of those nearby. They all looked spick-and-span; fresh off the boat. Max felt he could see the Army Manuals sticking out of their top pockets. They were as green as cabbage with about as much sense. Brainwashed. They'd probably shoot this chap themselves without a second's hesitation. Max stared them down.

'We must preserve the armed forces in a state of discipline!' exclaimed the padre as if he were endorsing the eleventh commandment. 'Disobedience, like measles, is so infectious that you cannot afford to run risks with it at all, and in war the individual is of small account. If one or two go by the board it is extremely unfortunate and sad but it cannot be helped. Although a man's nerve may break down we must look on it as a form of disgrace for a soldier, otherwise you would have everyone breaking down as soon as they wanted to go home. Examples must be made! If it can be done with justice, so much the better. But it must be done.'

Max sucked his teeth. There was no reasoning with a zealot, he thought to himself. And certainly not one confident of having God on his side. He offered the padre one of the two glasses of a treacly liquid purporting to be sherry that the mess corporal had brought over on a silver salver.

The padre lifted his nose. 'No thank you . . .'

Max smiled. 'The devil's water not to your taste?'

Evidently not, thought Max, masking the embarrassing silence by taking a sip of his own.

'How will he take it tomorrow?' he asked, inspecting his drink to check whether it was sherry or cough syrup.

The cleric looked away. 'Not well, I fear. He is young and so terribly frightened, so . . .'

His voice tailed off.

'Who would not be,' said Max. He pulled a face and, sweeping his palate with his tongue, placed the schooner of sticky brown liquid on a side table.

Then the two officers sat down to a supper of lamb chops, carrots and boiled potatoes for which neither could muster any enthusiasm. They sat in silence, prodding the food that swam in a watery excuse for gravy around their plates as if they were conducting imaginary manoeuvres for some forthcoming offensive.

As they took their leave of each other the padre put finger to mouth. 'One other thing, Lieutenant. Rather delicate. In the circumstances, the boy's CO wonders whether you might compose something for the next of kin?'

Max's face turned pink. 'I'll be buggered if I will!'

His nose quivered an inch from the startled padre's. 'It's bad enough being ordered to shoot the poor bastard on his account! I'm not bloody well salving his conscience—and yours—by writing to his mother as well!'

Then he stomped out.

4

Caulaincourt Chateau

Despite the luxury of a bed and a roof, Max slept fitfully and awoke scrabbling around the foot of the bed in search of Field Marshal Haig's day-book. He distrusted sleep, fearing it as death's mirror, and his slumbers, only ever two or three hours at a stretch, were invariably disrupted by lurid dreams bordering on the surreal. He would often wake in the grip of an hallucination and continue to live the dream for a minute or so. He slapped his cheeks and examined his surroundings to assure himself he was not running around Haig's HQ and that he was no *aide-de-camp*. But the significance of this subconscious reference to his being Haig's functionary was not lost on him.

Max brought his watch closer to his face. It was just after four o'clock. He rustled his hair and yawned, so hard his jaw cracked. He already felt exhausted and the day's ordeal had barely begun. He put a match to the oil lamp and pulled his breeches over his long johns. His toes curled on touching the damp floorboards before he could locate his socks and fight the cold by stamping into his boots. His feet felt as heavy as a box of ammo as he dragged them across to the wash-stand where a few splashes of cold water soon pin-pricked his senses to life. Jig-jogging on the spot, he emptied the rest of the jug into the bowl and shaved hurriedly by the mustard light of the lamp, managing to nick the corner of his mouth. He completed dressing with equal alacrity.

The only operation he conducted slowly was a methodical check of his revolver, squinting down the barrel and scrutinizing every bullet and chamber. He had gone over the moment innumerable times in his mind and the prospect of administering the *coup de race* got no easier. What if the poor blighter was still alive and his bullet had to do more than merely 'make sure'? He'd never killed a German in cold blood, nor so much as an animal. Putting a pistol to a human being's head didn't bear contemplation.

He tiptoed down the main staircase consumed by the bizarre need to be unheard and unseen as if he was some kind of hired assassin and exited into the chateau's courtyard to await the firing party's arrival. He had ordered Fenn to collect the men's rifles as soon as they had settled-in the previous evening. Now he loaded each of the .303 short magazine Lee-Enfields, putting live rounds into nine of them but, by custom, inserting a blank cartridge in the tenth. That way, each man might convince himself he was innocent of killing a comrade-in-arms.

The click-clack of boots on cobblestones that heralded the approach of the firing party resonated with the hollow sensation echoing around his stomach. Perhaps he ought to have fortified himself with some breakfast—as the padre advised—but the very thought of a slice of toast made him want to retch. How could he stomach breakfast when the poor bastard out in the stables whose life he was about to end was most probably emptying his.

He observed Fenn bring the men to attention. Some 15 yards distant, in front of a flint-stone wall, was a plain kitchen chair weighed down by sandbags; beside it lay a blanket and two ropes. On the other side of the wall, partially obscured by a mound of earth crowned with two shovels, was a freshly dug grave.

Max walked down the line, handing a rifle to each man, looking deep into his eyes as he did so. Bostock accepted his weapon with a knowing smile: he was sure Max would have put a 'live one up the spout' for him and he had made up his mind what he was going to do. Goodey accepted his with hands so clammy that it slipped through his fingers and would have clattered to ground had Max's reactions not been fast enough. Goodey could pot pigeons and rabbits for fun, not a thought spared for their suffering. But he wasn't so chirpy at the thought of dealing out death this morning. Max patted him on the forearm and took a second to straighten his tunic. It didn't need the attention; he felt its owner did.

Max sniffed and, in a monotone belying the mincer he felt was churning his guts to mush, he instructed them all to 'shoot straight and true . . . as a mercy to the condemned man . . . be humane . . . don't botch it.' He had grave doubts: they looked as if they'd all rather be queuing for de-lousing. He suspected some would shirk their duty and deliberately fire high.

The official witnesses marched into the yard. The Warwicks' commanding officer had decided against exercising his prerogative to have the execution carried out in front of the entire battalion. Instead, he had assembled one man and one subaltern to represent each platoon: there was much coughing and fingering of collars.

Max chewed his lower lip, clenched his gloved hands behind his back and then, just as involuntarily, unclenched and clenched them again. 'For Christ's sake,' he muttered to himself, 'let's get this over with.'

Every man in the yard heard the condemned man before they could see him. They knew the noise was man-made though it sounded scarcely human. It was a strange sound that reminded Max of a lost calf lowing for its mother: afraid; desperate; utterly pathetic. And as the first thin rays of spring sunlight began to inch across the cobblestones toward them, this pitiful noise only seemed to intensify.

A loose-box groaned ajar away to their right, causing every man in the firing party to stiffen as though stuck with a cattle prod. The jagged beam of light illuminated the padre standing in the doorway, head bowed, prayer book in hand, incanting the Service for the Dead: he licked his lips continually to ease the passage of words he trusted would be heard and answered by his God.

'Come on! Come on!' Max repeated under his breath as he felt an urge to pee taking hold. 'For pity's sake!'

He craned his neck and squinted into the light but still he failed to put human form to that desolate voice. Suddenly the poor wretch emerged, half-supported and half-dragged by two soldiers, the scraping of his hob-nailed boots over the cobblestones shattering the silence to an eerie firework display of yellow sparks. Behind him hovered the Regimental Medical Officer, lips also moving, praying his own role in the impending ritual would not extend beyond certifying that death was 'instantaneous.'

For his own part, Max prayed the condemned private had been reduced to this semi comatose state by the liberal tot of rum dispensed overnight and that he would eventually pass out. The alternative explanation was simpler and, he knew, much more likely. The man was just scared out of his wits.

The boy's face—because he looked no older than 15 or 16—appeared as if it already lay beneath its shroud, his red-rimmed eye sockets standing out like two wine stains on a pristine altar cloth: he had on him what the men called 'the thousand-yard stare', the glassy, empty-eyed gaze of a man who knew he was about to die. His mouth was twisted and half open, spittle dribbling down his chin and sticking to the few hairs dotting it; the livid welt on his left cheek presumably self-inflicted during a night of thrashing torment.

'Stand steady! Eyes front!' Max shouted.

Several rifle barrels wobbled nonetheless, their owners' resolve further weakened by the condemned begging them for mercy in a slurry of words rendered almost unintelligible by a mixture of tears, saliva and mucous.

The two escorts positioned him in the chair and bound his arms to its backrest and his ankles to its front legs. Max watched a stain darken the crotch of the soldier's khaki trousers and a trickle of liquid seep through his puttees to pool around his feet.

Max hoped the boy's senses were scrambled beyond the point of feeling humiliation. He forced himself to step forward and held his breath as a stench akin to a field latrine invaded his nostrils. He fished a length of white cloth from his pocket. The cloth snagged on its brass button. He tugged it free and wound it around the victim's eyes, securing it, at the second attempt, with a simple bow at the back of the head. Then he extricated a second, smaller, piece of cloth from his other pocket and began pinning it to the prisoner's chest: he could feel the boy's heart thumping beneath his fingers as he fought to push the pin through the coarse tunic and he began to panic at his ham-fistedness. He cursed his gloves for making his fingers behave like so many wet sponges and then winced as he pricked his thumb. Once more he swore under his breath, embarrassed and ashamed by his crassness.

Any vestige of human dignity seemed to have fled the condemned, but he must have felt some last knockings of fighting spirit because he raised his head and brought his lips up to Max's ear.

'Mother!' he whimpered. 'I wants me mother.'

Max blinked back a tear, envying the youth's faith in the healing powers of a maternal love that had always been a stranger to him.

He stepped back. The boy continued begging for his mother, though much less audibly. For the second time that morning Max quietly, self-consciously, cleared his throat.

'You'll soon be with her, old chap,' he whispered. 'Don't worry, it'll be fine.' With that, he patted him on the shoulder, straightened-up and strode back to the end of the firing-line. The tableau of death was in place.

He read out the death sentence, firm of voice and stance. Then he slowly raised his right arm. This was no occasion for shouted commands: a sequence of arm signals was standard procedure. Ten rifles rose, unsteadily as if too heavy for the arms that held them. Ten soldiers ordered to aim at one of their own. Whether each man did or did not, only each man would know. Max's flesh seemed to him to be melting and flooding into his boots. His focused his attention on a prominent flint on top of the wall that was catching the sun, and left his arm to gravity: it fell with the intransigence of a railway signal.

The volley was spasmodic, convincing Max some of the firing party had hesitated longer than others; but was still sufficient to blast man and chair sideways and send a line of crows roosting on the stable roof cawing skywards.

It brought an abrupt end to the condemned's wailing. But it had not killed him. Though Max could see blood spurting from his mouth and three separate wounds in his chest, the body continued to jerk, emitting a croaking death-rattle.

The RMO strode across purposefully, took a close look and shook his head. Max swore under his breath and, trying vainly to swallow the brick he felt lodged in his throat, walked over to join the RMO. He unclipped his holster, drew his revolver and bent over the trussed obscenity now reduced to writhing in its own excrement like some squashed and demented khaki spider.

Damn his men. Ten soldiers trained to stop a man in his tracks at 300 yards, aiming at a target just fifteen yards away, and they couldn't find the mark. Most of them had shot high on purpose. Damn them to hell. He glared at Bostock, lips whitening. If that bastard had put them up to it he was going to be brought to account.

Max looked down into the opaque eyes of an acne-ridden youth foolish enough to answer his country's call before his turn. His tongue probed the corner of his mouth, making the razor-nick sting like a thousand paper cuts. He licked his lips dry and ordered himself to carry on: this face rigid with terror before him could have passed for his own just a few years ago.

A chill gripped his backbone. It was as if the devil's dog had him in its jaws and was gnawing the life out of him. He sensed every eye staring at him, straining for any glimmer of weakness. He knew some observers would be willing him to falter, to crack.

As he had once before high up on the Black Bridge, Max Lanham felt his skin assume the clamminess of wet dough. He gulped for air and counted to three. Gently he squeezed the shoulder that lay beneath his left hand.

'It's all right, old man,' he said softly while positioning the muzzle of the Webley behind the boy-soldier's right ear until he could feel the barrel pressing against soft flesh. Then he turned his face away and pulled the trigger, spattering the boy's brains all over his cuff.

5

Lawn Upton Again

Max sprinted down the platform and jumped aboard the 2.10 from Oxford to Princess Risborough which would deposit him at Littlemore station in less than 15 minutes. He had not been home for almost a year. Once he'd been glad to get away. Now he was glad to be back.

God knows, he had no desire to fight and no wish to die. But the fate awaiting any of the 100,000 men targeted by Lord Kitchener's finger-jabbing 'Your Country Needs YOU!' ultimatum who rejected the call seemed infinitely worse. What young man wished to become an outcast, a pariah, a social leper; who wanted to be pointed out in the street as a 'shirker' or a 'scrim-shanker'? Everyone else in Exeter's quad that September morning in 1914 appeared so brave, so gung-ho, bursting with patriotism, jingoism even. He had to confront his fears. It was only after volunteering that he discovered everyone else was equally petrified. And, anyway, as they re-assured themselves, the 2nd Battalion was only raised for home defence after the 1st was ordered overseas: signing the Imperial Service Obligation which committed them to follow seemed merely academic.

Their war began in Port Meadow with endless drilling using brooms and hoes for Rifles followed by month after month under canvas while digging land defences in Essex. Then, in late 1915, news of escalating casualty rates at the front began filtering through, along with rumours of a major 'push' aimed at breaking the stalemate of trench warfare along a line from the River Somme in the south to Ypres in the north. The bush telegraph was correct: in January 1916 the 650-strong battalion was dispatched to Parkhouse Camp on Salisbury Plain to be made up for foreign service. Three months later 2nd Lieutenant Max Lanham marched his platoon past His Majesty King George V and onto the train that would take them to Folkestone and France. Within a week of arriving in the Fauquissart sector, east of Laventie, they came under artillery fire. And it had barely ceased ever since.

Max's one-carriage train struggled across the bridge spanning the River Thames, its ironwork black with layers of soot and smoke, that signalled the approach of Littlemore Station. He dropped the sash and lent out of the window, and felt a blast of cool air freshen his cheeks. He searched the bridge for a glimpse of anyone clinging to the girders but spotted no one.

He wondered if Chick Collicutt was among this season's jumpers. His head wobbled with a suppressed chuckle. Chick old enough to jump off the Black Bridge. It beggared belief. It seemed only yesterday he couldn't tie his boot laces properly. Max would know soon enough because Littlemore was too small a place for everyone not to know each other's business; indeed the villagers felt it more prerogative than intrusion. Much as he hated to acknowledge the probability, every family in the village doubtless knew he was coming home today—and on which train. 'Please God,' he muttered. 'Let there be no welcoming committee.'

Only Sherriffs was there to greet him. Max pressed a sixpenny bit into his hand as the porter went to help him with his kit, explaining that Mr Pomeroy sends his compliments and apologies for not being present. Max was perfectly happy in see the station master in absentia and began trudging up the steep rise from the station overlooked by the County Lunatic Asylum. This grim edifice, redolent of a prison than a hospital, guarded the southern approach to the village much as the vast bulk of the Oxford Sanitary Steam Laundry (and its mighty chimney) protected the northern side. He bore right over the bridge and walked down toward The George Inn; from the adjoining smithy he heard the tuneless clang of hammer against iron.

Albert Bostock sixth-sensed Max's presence and, looking up, proceeded to plunge the pincered horseshoe into the quench bucket. The frothing water whooshed to a hiss but failed to drown the blacksmith's words of greetings because there were none: only a cursory drop of the head that no one could ever confuse with so much as a welcoming nod. The blacksmith thrust the shoe back into the fire.

Max would've been shocked by any other reaction. The Jesuit boast 'give us the child and we'll give you the man' always came to mind whenever he dealt with Hector Bostock because he was the absolute incarnation of his blacksmith father: both flaxen-haired six-foot oblongs of muscle blessed with their trade's overdeveloped right forearm, both capable in a past life, Max often thought, of doing valiant service among King Harold's axe-wielding 'house-carls' at the Battle of Hastings.

Max kept on walking, irritated by the odd pang of guilt at not conveying news to a father of his soldier-son's continued well-being, and yet pleased he'd kept faith with his conscience. He hoped the squat red-brick cottage opposite might offer a warmer welcome and squinted into the sun for any sign of its occupant. He thought he saw a swirl of hair and stopped, waiting and praying it might reappear. But it was a false dawn. The window remained minus picture.

Max inhaled his disappointment. He had not been back in Littlemore barely five minutes and he was already starting to wish he was somewhere else. And he had not even reached home yet.

He stopped at the gates of Lawn Upton. At the rear of the lodge Mrs Goodey was hanging out her washing: she dropped her basket and rushed over to hug him. She told him how well he looked and he assured her of Arthur's health and enquired after her husband. After protracting the conversation for as long as he felt able, his eyes went to the top of the drive and he felt his gizzards start to churn as if he were stood on the fire-step awaiting the whistle to go over the top.

The view itself had never failed to lift his spirits whenever he came home from boarding school. There before him was a beautiful cream-stone manor house resplendent with three tall chimney stacks, the family crest of a heron clearly visible on the right-hand gable above his personal bolt hole, the library, from whose French windows he might gaze across the expanse of grass that led the eye toward the spinney and its promise of a cooler reading spot on humid summer afternoons. He glanced up at the bow-window below the crest (as much to check that his bedroom was still there) before putting his shoulder against the heavy arched door and giving the iron-ringed handle a hefty wrench—which, as usual, saw him almost fall into the hallway. He dropped his valise on the dipping flagstone floor but any temptation to turn right into the library was frustrated by the drawing room door opening.

'Oh, Max! I thought it must be you! Come and give your mother a kiss!'

Naomi Lanham offered her only son each cheek in turn and he obliged her, if not quite sinking to the grimacing reluctance of a nephew honouring a hairy-chinned maiden aunt, demonstrating a pursed-lipped refusal to make full affectionate contact.

His mother's hands slid down to his as she took a step back.

'How are you? You appear full of health,' she said admiringly. 'As good as new, hardly a scratch on you. We do worry about you so. Why don't you write more often?'

'A new gown, I see,' he said. 'Raiding Elliston and Cavell again?'

'Don't tease!' she smirked, tapping the back of his hand.

To Max this show of polite affection was as demeaning as his reaction was vicious. 'Who'd have thought your father tended pigs . . .'

'I see the war has done nothing for your manners!' his mother replied. Her expression had barely altered. She lived in the present and planned for the future. The past was dead to her. If only her son would allow it to stay that way.

'. . . and to think all you've ever done to earn such finery was sell fruit and veg in the Covered Market!'

'I run this house . . .'

'Did I mishear you?' Max snapped. 'Shouldn't that be "*rule* this house"?'

Naomi Lanham tweaked her head to one side and patted her hips, waiting for her son's pique to subside. Then she might start all over again as if nothing had happened.

'But it is a gorgeous frock, isn't it? I bought it especially for you . . . your homecoming! You're all mine now for, what, seven—no five, I suppose, with the travelling—whole glorious days! Let's sit down in the drawing room and chat about our plans, shall we?'

Max manufactured a wintry smile and tried to break free but her grip belied her delicacy: a freakish strength that called to mind those female insects who consume their mates after love-making. She dragged him toward the *chaise longue* and Dickens's image of Sydney Carton in his tumbrel bound for the guillotine suddenly drove all others from his mind. The thought forced a chuckle out of him.

'It's so refreshing to see you still able to laugh!' she said. 'So rewarding after all you must have endured.'

Max kept the source of his mirth to himself, which only made him chuckle louder. 'You know me, mother. Resilient! Put up with anything I can. A stoic if ever there was.'

His facetiousness was lost on his mother for her mental acuity came nowhere near her physical powers. It seemed he could say anything to her, and yet within an instant the slight would be forgotten or forgiven—the former, he guessed, because he'd seen too many staff dismissed and family friends ostracized to think she believed in the latter. He pondered a further witticism, but hadn't the energy. Since there was no blackboard and chalk available for him to spell out in big letters what it felt like to put a bullet in the brain of a half-dead teenage boy in the name of military justice and be granted home leave as a result, he contented himself with asking the whereabouts of his father.

'You must have passed him. Down at the lodge, I imagine, talking horses with Goodey. That's all he ever seems to do!'

She tapped the velvet seat beside her. 'Come and sit next to your mother. I've a lovely surprise for you!'

Max could see Carton ascending that scaffold and hear him muttering something like 'It is a far, far better thing that I do . . .' as he did her bidding. For God's sake, he prayed, don't let it be a homecoming party.

'I've arranged a drinks party this evening to welcome my hero home!' she trilled. 'Just a few friends—and one or two local people of substance . . .'

'The sort of people who brighten up a room by leaving it?'

Her shoulders stiffened and the wide-mouthed smile, staged, he had no doubt, for his benefit and reciprocation, fled as swiftly as it came.

'You don't appear especially grateful,' she said in a voice frosty enough to burn fingers.

Max got up and walked to the window. 'First of all, I'm no hero . . .'

'Don't be so modest . . .'

Max picked up a Wemyss pottery pig from the Sheraton side table, weighed it thoughtfully and considered smashing it to the floor. Instead he turned to face the enemy.

'Very well, then,' he said, holding up the figurine as some kind of intermediary, 'to tell the truth, meeting "a few friends" and "local people of substance"—as you call them—is the last way I would like to spend my first evening home.'

'But you must!' said his mother, prising the porcelain figurine from his fingers. 'There are people you should meet. People who will prove extremely useful to you once the war is over. There's Mr Amor from the Hospital . . .'

'At least he's used to making small talk with half-wits!'

'Why must you be so obnoxious! It's simply uncalled for!' she replied, mouth hardening into a thin red gash. 'If you must know, the asylum is currently in service as a war hospital.'

Max's cheeks turned a shade deeper than her lipstick. 'Oh . . .'

'And I do so want you to talk with the chairman of the parish council . . .'

'God, no!' blurted out Max, all embarrassment banished. 'Not Tinegate again!'

'Mr Amor and Mr Tinegate have been invited—and they've accepted. You can't let me down. What will people think?'

Max did not give a farthing what people might think even if his mother did.

'And Vanessa will be coming . . .'

'Christ Almighty, not Vanessa Devereux as well!' moaned Max, gripping the window ledge in exasperation.

'I knew you'd consider the whole thing rather stuffy and might need company. She had another engagement but I persuaded her—well, she needed little persuasion—to come.'

'All tweeds and meaty hips, a bell in every tooth . . .' Max mumbled. '. . . that snooty gasbag has a lot to answer for!'

He stared out through the window toward the glade and saw her as plain as the afternoon he spent hiding in one of the chestnut trees after his attempts to dislodge conkers with a stick only succeeded in knocking her on the head. She had howled like a banshee and he received a thrashing from his mother. That was the last tree he ever climbed: heights and terror had been inextricably linked ever since. And a morbid belief in the inevitability of retribution and punishment.

Max groaned. 'Mother, how many times do I have to tell you . . .'

'She's pretty . . .'

'Shouldn't I be the judge of that? She looks like a hyena that's swallowed a hatchet!' terrible company!'

His mother rubbed the snout of the pig with a manicured finger tip.

'No sense of humour whatsoever! Boring as hell!' Max ground out between gritted teeth. 'She'll bang on and on about Einstein's theory of relativity or his new crackpot views about gravity!'

'She is the only child of a very, very good family . . .'

'A wealthy family, you mean!'

'Cynicism does not become you, Max!'

'I had a fine teacher!'

'How dare you speak to your mother in that tone of voice!' she said, tapping the pig up and down on its table.

'I'd be careful with that pig, mother, he's priceless and you'll have his tail off,' smirked Max. 'And, just for the record, what tone might that be?'

'There it is again,' she countered with a toss of the head. 'That tone. Disrespectful, ungrateful, not an ounce of love.'

Max was about to release the beast he felt shaking the bars of his breast when he heard the door open behind him.

'Max! You're home! How are you?'

Roy Lanham shuffled the three steps across the room to greet his son as tentatively as if he were traversing a minefield, unable to decide whether to offer his hand or an embrace. In the event he did neither. And instantly regretted it. He was the boy's father. His first role model. His most important role model. He ought to take the initiative. It troubled him that he could not. It troubled him that he had never been able to find the courage to show his son love. Neither in word nor action.

Max watched his father dither and knew exactly what ailed him because he was wrestling with the same predicament, those same old questions. Who would make the first move? Should he? Christ Almighty, the Old Man was more repressed than he was. So that reduced the possible volunteers to one.

Max had spent that short train journey from Oxford mulling over ways of healing the emotional detachment that crippled his relationship with his father. How hard could it be to embrace him, to wrap arms around him and plant a son's gentle and respectful kiss on his cheek? He knew every day at the front might be his last and that every opportunity to do so might be the final opportunity. Yet even with this sword of Damocles to hand, he could not find a way of slicing through the knotted emotions that continued to hobble him.

'Find Rufey and ask her to bring us some tea, will you. I'm discussing something rather important with Max.'

The worry-lines left Max's forehead. As usual his mother had taken control. Problem solved. Or at least sidelined. Father and son stood their ground, each feeling ashamed at the palpable sense of relief they both felt.

'I'm fine, father. And you?'

'Fine . . . fine,' was the best he could offer in mumbled reply. 'Best get that tea organized.'

It was a physical impossibility for blood to boil in his veins but Max felt its pressure rising in his temples. 'Father! Come straight back, won't you? I want to pick your brains about the Leger. Is Gay Crusader the certainty they say he is?'

A light suddenly shone behind Roy Lanham's eyes and he seemed to grow an inch taller. 'Right you are, Max. Goodey and I were only saying this morning . . .'

'Roy, please don't forget the tea. Max must be parched!'

'Yes,' he replied, shoulders crumpling. 'Of course.'

Max turned back to his mother, primed to antagonize. 'Granny Jake coming to this party of yours?'

The question detonated with the impact of a German 5.9. His mother's single-word response in the negative took an age to frame and articulate, as Max suspected it would.

'At her age it's such a long journey from Cowley,' she explained after taking some seconds to pat down some supposedly errant hair in her chignon.

'You could send the car . . .'

'No, my mother's far too frail,' she added in a stronger voice. 'In any case, it would be too noisy for her.'

Max looked up at the portraits of Herbert and Mildred Lanham staring at each other from the alcoves on either side of the fireplace knowing there was no point searching the room for any similar homage to his other grandparents. Of Ernest and Jane Jacobson there was no trace: no paintings; not photographic portrait; not even a snap shot.

He shrugged. 'I think I'll go and unpack and then jump into a hot bath if I'm to attend a party. I'm not really ready for any tea. I'll drop into the kitchen as I go and inform Rufey.'

'But Max, we've not finished our chat . . .'

Her son was already half-way through the door.

'Max, you will wear your dress uniform tonight, won't you?'

Max stopped. 'Sorry, mother. Didn't bring it. Travelled light. No room. You and your distinguished guests will have to make do with khaki. But don't panic I'll put some spit n' polish on these mucky boots for you!'

Then he closed the door behind him and climbed the stairs with a clownish grin on his face.

6

The Glade

The hubbub coming from the library caused Max to pause at the bottom of the stairs and contemplate whether he had the stomach for what lay ahead. Straightening his tie and tucking his cap under his left arm, he sucked in his chest and strode in to find himself engulfed by a round of applause. He cringed and forced a smile while nodding his gratitude. On the plus side, there was no sign of Vanessa Devereux: that much he could be sure because she would have been hanging on his lapels by now with the obstinacy of a staff officer's red tabs.

'So how are things going over there? Giving Fritz hell?'

Max stared at Henry Amor and saw a caricature of a Little Englander. He wondered whether this event could feasibly plumb any lower depths. Accepting a glass of sherry from the tray Rufey suspended in front of him, he looked into the pop-eyes of the rotund sexagenarian stood beside her. 'In actual fact, Mr Amor, if you must know, we're giving each other hell.'

'But I imagine theirs is a mite hotter, eh?' Amor sniggered at his own joke.

'You imagine?' replied Max testily. 'I imagine you have never seen service?'

Amor failed to detect the edge in Max's voice. 'Territorials in '83 in Norfolk, Thetford it was.'

'You will never imagine what it's truly like to be under fire, continuously, 24 hours of the day, unless you've been obliged to endure it.'

'Why, of course,' interjected Horace Bowler, manager of the laundry, 'but exhilarating all the same? The camaraderie, seeing the whites of the Hun's eyes and putting him to the sword, just like we cavalrymen put paid to those infernal Boers!'

Max felt the rhomboid muscles at the top of his back tighten as if in the grip of a giant hand. If they want the unvarnished truth, he thought, they shall have it.

'No man, however he may talk, has the remotest idea of what today's ordinary infantryman really goes through. It's a war with no glamour or glory. Modern weapons are too deadly . . .'

'Of course, my boy, of course.'

'The theatre of war has altered beyond all recognition . . .'

'Indeed, it must have.'

Words tumbled from Max's mouth faster and faster. 'There's nothing vaguely heroic about this war. You never see the whites of anyone's eyes except the terrified ones belonging to your own men! There's none of your dashing charges and flashing sabres. There's almost no movement whatsoever. It's long range combat. Three out of four men, Mister Bowler, are killed by artillery.'

'Oh, really?' Bowler harrumphed, crestfallen.

'I should rather say blown to smithereens by gigantic guns. Our 18-pounders versus their 420s, hurling enormous shells at men, as lousy as rooks, hiding in holes in the ground until their nerves are smashed or they can hope to mount an attack over open ground without the risk of being shredded by machine-gun fire. And for what? We're like two boxers in an endless clinch, wrestling an inch here, conceding one there . . .'

Max's father edged slowly through the guests toward his son. He'd never worn a uniform but he recognized fear in a man when he saw it. The brightness in the eye incompatible with the darkness of the words; the jerky arms atop stiff legs. However, it was his wife who reached Max first. She looped an arm round his and tried to usher him aside but she found him as immobile as a howitzer.

'I'm sure all our guests have grasped your meaning,' she said, addressing Max with a moistness of eye that if beheld in others he would have accepted as heartfelt. 'We're all so proud of you! I think I can say that on behalf of everyone here. None more so than your father and I.'

There was a murmur of assent but if it was meant to censor or silence Max it failed. He closed his eyes as if trying to recall the opening lines of a poem.

'One night I came upon one of my men lying in a shell hole, cradling his tin hat in his arms. He had a huge smile on his face and was rocking the hat to and fro, talking to it as if it were his baby.'

'Shell shock?' ventured Amor.

'A man's courage is his capital and he is always spending,' droned Max as if he was back in that shell hole with Ted Goodchild. 'This war's about power and money, yet it's the ordinary folk who are paying the price. And when a man is spent out he is finished.'

'Can't say I've any time for this shell-shock business!'

Max swivelled in the direction of the intervention and beheld Norman Tinegate. How he loathed such men as he, men whose modicum of success in one field—in Tinegate's case Littlemore's sawmill in Railway Lane—convinced them their opinion mattered in all others; men who gloried in their ordinariness and made a virtue of their pomposity. Tinegate stood there in his crisp new shirt that looked as if it had come straight out of the Shepherd & Woodward packaging and a dark suit that wore him rather than vice versa, sporting the sort of permanently self-satisfied expression that made Max wish he had a custard pie secreted behind his back ready to shove into his face.

'The term should be abolished! The quacks are making fear respectable. The men are getting to know the term. I've read all about it!'

'Have you now?'

'Yes, I certainly have! Cases are multiplying. It's getting out of hand. The men are even telling the quacks when they've got it!'

'Are they indeed.'

'Cowards of this sort are a serious danger to the army. Shell-shock's nothing less than self-preservation and the fear of being found afraid. It's blasted scrim-shanking, I tell you!'

Max tried to fix Tinegate's piggy eyes with a slaughter-man's glare but they proved too shifty.

'It is inconceivable how men who have pledged themselves to fight and uphold the honour of their country could degrade themselves and show an utter want of that manly spirit and courage which is expected of every soldier and Britisher.'

Max felt himself start to tremble: he sensed where Tinegate's diatribe was leading. Those closest to Max noticed and surreptitiously nudged each other.

'Fear is infectious! It breeds terror! It influences others!'

Tinegate sipped his whisky and sniffed. 'Don't misunderstand me . . .'

Here it comes, muttered Max under his breath as soon as he recognized the usual tap-room bore's preamble to some worthless screed.

'. . . but I say, shoot a few! The death penalty is there to make men fear running away more than they fear the enemy! These men are degenerates. No better than conscientious objectors, these conchies that are running around the place.'

'And that, Mr Tinegate, is your considered opinion?'

'Yes, it is,' said Tinegate, jutting out his jaw at 45 degrees. 'They've not all got your guts!'

Max giggled. 'Do you want to hear about guts, Mr Tinegate? Would you like to hear something of these cowards you mention and what they have to contend with on a daily basis?'

'Now, Max,' said his mother, squeezing his arm, 'don't darken the mood.'

Max shook his arm free and, this time, pursued Tinegate's eyes until their owner felt as if a new ice cube had formed in his glass of Scotch.

'Do you remember a boy named Albert Lones?'

'The dairyman's lad out at Minchery Farm?'

'Yes, that's Albert—Baggy to his friends, of whom I was one.'

'Really?' said Tinegate out of the side of his mouth.

Max's eyes shone with an emotional dew. His mother observed it from behind her fan which steadily rose in front of her face to conceal blackening eyes. She had tried to save Max from himself but he would not listen. He would never be told.

'Well, let me tell you about Baggy. One night we were out in front on a working party, strengthening a sap and laying wire, standard sort of thing. Fritz soon gets to know about it . . . hears the shovels hitting stones and so on. He swamps the sky with star shells and pretty soon the creeping barrage of shells starts up. In the lights the blasts send up this eerie white smoke, a haze reminiscent of a London pea-souper. By God, when you hear those shells getting closer and closer you're convinced the next one'll drop straight on your head. But it's pointless running. Where can you run to? You might run straight into one.'

Max's voice cut through the room like shrapnel.

'So we all hit the ground, searching for even the slightest cavity in which to bury our heads, lying there hoping the next one goes over, listening for the next blast and praying it'll be the last, as if you're sitting in the dentist's chair longing for the drilling to stop, listening for the sound of steel as it goes by you, the dreadful whine of a piece of steel that could cut you in two.'

The words began to dry on Max's tongue, his voice becoming sand-lined in its huskiness.

'Baggy was out front wire-laying . . .'

Tinegate moved closer. 'Go on, man.'

'A lone shell burst over head, it was a trench mortar, a *minenwerfer*, the men call them "minnywoffers", big bastards they are . . .'

'Max! There are ladies present!'

Max ignored his mother's entreaty.

'Real bastards!' he repeated with extra venom for her benefit. 'They don't make a sound, you see, when they're dispatched. If you don't catch the sound of the warning whistle being blown by the Boche gunners before they fire them, the first thing you are likely to know about it is seeing this object like a tumbling pigeon falling toward you. Then it's woof, woof, woof . . .'

As Max's voice rose to a lupine pitch his mother flicked open her fan and attempted to engage Edith Amor in conversation rather than watch her son make an exhibition of himself.

'. . . jagged strips of metal whirring through the air, tearing to shreds anything in its path. Anyway, we got back up again and scraped the mud and gubbins off our faces . . .'

Max's brain wandered hundreds of miles to the east and registered only the chatter of machine-gun fire and the cries of terrified men. His face twisted as he struggled to form his words.

'There was this . . . shadow . . . shape . . . on the wire. Hanging there like a piece of Ada Goodey's washing.'

'Dead Hun?' prompted Tinegate.

'No, it was . . .'

Max's hands began clawing at the invisible demons he felt pricking his cheeks with their tridents. But he could not make them stop. He would have to retreat. He walked briskly from the room, head down, not daring to look left nor right. He glimpsed his mother's mouth opening and closing in protest but it was that sight resembling a butcher's shop window which left him quaking: the image of a piece of meat hanging from the wire that might have been a leg of lamb but was Baggy Lones's left arm. They knew it was his on account of the letters B.A.G.G.Y tattooed on the knuckles of the fingers gripping the wire like a line of fish hooks; but there was no sign of the other hand that carried L.O.N.E.S.—or any other part of him. The next day they bulked the ground sheet with stones for his burial. Max was haunted by the fact it was bits of his friend not mud that had splattered his face that night.

Max sought the sanctuary of the glade. He gazed up into the branches swishing patterns across the sapphire canvas of the night sky and began shaking as they described the mortal remains of Baggy Lones impaled on the wire. He gripped the nearest tree and threw up. He wiped his mouth with the back of his hand and stared at the trunk. There were the initials he and Baggy Lones had carved with their penknives.

He looked up at the moon and wanted to howl.

7

Railway Lane

Max pushed himself away from the tree. He staggered across the grass, gathering pace as he put more distance between himself and the tangible reminder of Baggy Lones. He was running in search of solace. He knew where he wanted to find it.

He saw a light in the bedroom window of the cottage on the corner of Railway Lane. Creeping through the gate, he tip-toed past the front door overgrown with honeysuckle and felt his way round to the back door, just as the front door opened and a thick-set figure exited. The man looked about him and crossed the road toward the smithy.

Max took a tight hold of the handle and slowly eased the back door open. He slipped his body sideways through the narrow opening into the pitch dark and counted off the three steps before he had to edge left if he was not to bump into the table. He had not, however, taken into account the needs of the cat who shot through the gap alongside him and wound up entangled between his legs.

The ensuing crash of pots and crockery soon brought the light of a lamp. 'Who's there? I'll shout for 'elp!'

The flash of light made Max dive onto the floor, arms protecting his head, stomach pressed hard to the floor, boots scrambling like a climber seeking footholds. 'Zena!' he called. 'It's only me! Sorry!'

The light hovered overhead. 'Max, issat you?'

'Blasted moggy of yours nearly caused me a mischief!' he complained, blinking into the foggy oil lamp while slowly getting to his feet.

'My God, Zena,' he said as the lamp bathed her in a sepulchral glow. 'You are so incredibly beautiful.'

Zena Boas was not unaccustomed to hearing that she possessed the kind of aura that drove cavemen to chisel on rock walls, and however reluctant she was to believe in their sincerity, she had been obliged in time to acknowledge their authenticity.

When she inspected her face in the mirror she saw perfectly symmetrical, finely sculpted features—though she felt her mouth was too big and her nose too pert—and the brunette hair she brushed out was long and lustrous. As for her body, it made her as happy as any woman has a right to be: the breasts she held up, felt full, firm and generously tipped; the belly she held in, already so flat as made no difference; the legs she smoothed, long and toned. She was the spark and tinder for every young man in the village, and a fair few of their fathers as well.

Max had been mesmerized the moment he first saw her: in Lawn Upton's scullery, sat over a bucket of potatoes, a paring knife in one hand, a half-peeled potato in the other. When she looked up and smiled it was as if someone had lit a fire in his loins. Whenever there was a dinner party thereafter and he knew Mrs Tedder would be in need of help preparing the vegetables, he would make some excuse to go down into the kitchen. He soon learnt the girl's name, but it took some wheedling to find out that she was only a year older than he and that she lived alone, making ends meet, as she told him, 'best as I can.' On his fifteenth birthday he asked her to marry him; she giggled and told him 'not a be so silly.' On his seventeenth birthday she took his virginity, tenderly and without laughing. He told her that had she been born with the social advantages of Vanessa Devereux she would be lady to a rich man and the mistress of a fine household; again she laughed in his face, but this time it was more coquettish. 'Pr'aps one o' these days I'll find a proper gentleman,' she said, stroking his cheek. When she saw him in uniform, going off to war, all too late she believed she had.

'Still here, then?' he said.

'An' you're still as gormless! Wossit it look loik!'

'I thought some sensible chap might have snapped you up.'

'Oh, one of those posh blokes who's goin' to come down here an' carry me of on the back o' a white horse? Fat chance o' that!'

In spite of the elocution lessons Max had tried to give her betwixt love-making Zena still spoke with the same Thames Valley accent as his men. But unlike the drone of his platoon that drummed holes in his brain, Zena's burr awoke his sentimental side and soothed. She had long since given up the struggle, deciding that any improvement in her pronunciation or grammar would never vanquish the embarrassment that keeps people in their proper place. What distinguished her 'betters', she concluded, was that measure of inherent self-esteem which made them so at ease with themselves. No amount of advancement on her part could replicate that.

'Iss all right for Mr Bernard Shaw to write a fairy story loik that *Pygmalian* you gave me to read, but fairy stories don't 'appen in Littlemore!'

Max could only shrug in silent agreement. But he wished they did.

'I heard you wuz home,' she said, setting the lamp down in the centre of the kitchen table. 'But I didn't s'pect to see you tonight. What with all the comin' an' goin' at your place.'

She straightened and effected her version of a posh accent. 'I knew it had to be for some sort of welcome-home party.'

'Some welcome party!' Max replied through down-turned mouth. 'I couldn't stay there another minute . . .'

'Second best, then, am I?' she laughed.

Max held her by the elbows. 'Don't you ever say such a thing. You ought to know better. Haven't I told you often enough . . .'

Zena cupped his face in her hands. 'Come to bed, Max.'

It was an order not an invitation, issued softly and franked with a kiss. Max inhaled the faint musk of sex and felt the warmth of her mouth re-activate every libidinous nerve-end in his body after months of lassitude. She picked up the lamp and led him through the door and up the stairs to her bedroom.

'I'll just be a minute,' she said, depositing the lamp on the dresser, beside a small tower of half-crowns. She saw Max spy the pile of coins and reach into his pocket.

'No!' she said sharply, aquamarine eyes glistening. 'There's never been any call for that! An' you knows it!'

Max reddened, ashamed.

He undressed, smoothed out the sheet and climbed into the bed, bouncing up and down to test the springs and see if they still squeaked like a row of hungry piglets. He chuckled, but only briefly as he wondered how many times they had squeaked since he last exercised them. But Zena had to live; she had to eat; she had to find the rent to pay Albert Bostock from somewhere.

She came back to him smelling faintly of soap and happy memories, lifted the bedspread and slid on top of him. She had one thought uppermost in her mind: to make love to him as though he was her first man of the day and they were a pair of lusting teenagers. She smiled when she heard him moan, pleased to be teasing the tension from his body and chasing the troubles from his brain.

'I can't go back there Zena,' he said afterward as he lay in the crook of her arm, her breast his pillow. 'Every second seems like a minute, every minute an hour.'

'Your party?'

'No, the front.'

'Oh,' she said, stroking his hair. 'So all the stories are true? It is hell out there.'

'It's hard to describe the horror, Zena, it really is . . .'

'Then don't try,' she said, kissing him on the cheek.

He couldn't help himself. 'Just imagine yourself up on Wittenham Clumps, looking down on the Thames valley, to Chipping Hampden or Dorchester, huddled round their quaint churches and taverns.'

She felt his body tightening and cuddled him harder, hoping he would stop talking.

'Then batter the scene with a giant sledgehammer, day and night, until almost every landmark has been obliterated. Strip it of every vestige of greenery—every hedgerow, every tree, every blade of grass. Smash holes in those churches. Pound the entire landscape into a putty-coloured wilderness. Nothing but mile on mile of emptiness. And then watch it pour with rain, torrential thunderstorms which transform it into an ocean of mud, mud like you've never imagined. To walk in it is like trying to wade through caramel toffee. You have to wrench your foot out of the morass every step of the way so that even ten yards reduce your leg muscles to jelly.'

'You poor dear,' she said, placing a finger to his lips. 'Don't say any more, please.'

Max pushed her finger away.

'When you're in the line your home is a three-feet deep slit in the earth, probably no more than a couple of feet wide,' he said calmly. 'If you're lucky there's a dug-out cut into a wall for shelter when the bombardment starts or when you dare to snatch some sleep.'

Life started to course through Max like a foal rising to its feet. 'Most of the men have to sleep where they sit, hunched like some animal, or stood up, propped against their rifles. Your life is sustained by tins—Maconochie stew, bully beef and jam—and hard tack biscuits fit to break any molars. Even the simple pleasure of a mug of tea is denied us . . . the water is ferried up to us in old petrol cans and if no one's had the time to burn them out properly you get a mouthful of something closer to petrol than tea! We pray that the rum ration arrives. Without it—and the letters from home—I don't know how we'd cope.'

Zena could feel his heart thumping against her belly and the horror he was reliving began to frighten her into clinging onto him even more tightly.

'Imagine the vilest stench you've ever smelt and then double it, no treble it, and you'll get some idea of the stink in those oozing trenches we must call home. The impossibility of keeping one's clothes dry and getting one's body clean. The ignominy of having to be de-loused regularly. Your body aches from sheer physical and nervous exhaustion but you can get no peace. If you're not lying awake scratching from the lice you're playing hide and seek with rats as big as cats! We live minute to minute. You see the sun come up, and you're grateful to see it set. You're either dead or you're alive. If you're alive, there's no need to worry. If you're dead, you're past worrying. So why worry?'

Max began to shake, his chest first, then his limbs and finally his cheeks. Zena pushed herself up onto her elbows to look at him. He was not crying but laughing.

'And do you know the funniest thing?'

'Max, please,' she begged. 'Stop upsettin' yourself.'

'No, really, let me tell you. Please!' he said, sitting up to face her. 'You get used to seeing the dead bodies, all bloated and green. But you must never mention a dead comrade. You dare not or you'd never stand it . . . be able to carry on. You must forget . . . become hardened.'

Max rested his hands on her shoulders. 'Let me give you an example. One day we came upon this corpse lying half-buried in the bottom of a trench and it was impossible to pass by without stepping on him. And do you know what? Every time we trod on the bugger his tongue would come out! It was hilarious! By the time the tenth man went over him old Fritz must have heard our laughter it was so loud!'

'Max, I think you oughter get some sleep. I'll fetch you some warm milk.'

'Two thousand years after Christ came to save us,' he said vacantly, 'and we can't do better than try to kill each other.'

But she'd gone. She returned with the milk and held it up to his lips. He just rolled onto his back, locking his hands behind his neck.

'My platoon is an absolute bloody nightmare. During officer training they hammer it into you to get to know your men because men are the first weapon of battle: "Know your men, Mister Lanham, and they'll follow you anywhere!" Well, I knew most of mine before I started. Seemed half of Littlemore had joined up and they assigned the bloody lot of them to my platoon. Wanley, Pulker, Pitson, Dewe, Goodey . . .'

'An' Bostock.'

'Yes, mustn't forget bloody Bostock!'

'Still a troublemaker?'

Max stared straight ahead. 'You see, they didn't tell you there might be a problem if your men knew you as well as you were meant to know them!'

Max sat up, and drank the milk in one draught. 'Do you know, I'm ashamed to say that stood down, in billets or in reserve, I've grown to hate them. Their petty crime, their stubborn moods, the continual bad language.'

'They're just afraid, Max. We're all God's creatures . . .'

'Yes, even the Germans!' snorted Max.

'X'actly.'

'What unites us is being under fire. And, unbelievably, they look to me for some kind of leadership. They have that frightened and rather piteous look of wonder in the eyes that seems to be asking: "Why are we here? Why are these monstrous shells being dropped on us? Sir, can't you order them to stop?" Well, I can't! Because we're trapped in a game organized by lunatics. Organized murder!'

She knew of only one way to soothe him. Prising the empty cup from his hands and placing it on the floor, she began kissing and licking his chest until he was ready to make love a second time.

'No human being knows how sweet sleep is but a soldier,' he replied after awaking from a slumber free of ghouls and sweaty underclothes. 'One night I was in such a state that I woke to find myself stood against a wall, preparing to repel an imaginary attack!'

'You poor dear,' she whispered, massaging his shoulders, 'you must be glad to be home?'

Max arched his head away.

'The words "glad" and "home" in the same sentence set my teeth on edge,' he muttered. 'I thought you'd know that by now.'

She wrapped her arms around his chest and once again felt his trembling.

'Zena, I've just come back from a hell on earth,' he said, twisting to look her in the eye. 'You'd think, in any normal family, that would be cause for thanking God, for parents and son to rejoice, for them to leap into each other's arms out of sheer relief, if not love. So, why can't my mother cuddle me without giving the impression of being a praying mantis? Why can't I hug my father without feeling a fraud?'

Zena stroked his hair and rocked him back and forth. 'It's a shame you never 'ad a brother or a sister . . .'

Max jerked upright. 'She hadn't enough love for me, so finding some for a brother would've taxed her!'

'But youder loved one?'

'Of course,' said Max, lowering his voice. 'Always longed for a brother. I'd even have put up with a sister!'

Zena waited for the moment to pass. 'It was thoughtful of her, though, to welcome you with a party.'

She felt Max convulse with laughter.

'That wasn't a welcome party! It was a showing-off party! "Here everybody! Look at my gallant son, in his spiffing uniform, fresh from serving his country proud!" All part of my mother's grand plan.'

'You make her sound like the Kaiser! She's not that bad, surely?'

'Let me show you the other side of my sainted mother. When I went away to school and learnt to fend for myself I asked that I might bath myself when I came home at weekends and during the holidays. It was that time of a boy's life when he wants to keep his body to himself, or at least away from the prying eyes of his mother. She agreed, but only if I left the bathroom door unlocked in case of emergencies.'

'Sounds reas'nable . . .'

'Every bath night she made some excuse to come and check on me!' continued Max, his voice growing harder with every word. 'I used to feel her eyes examining every inch of me like a dried-up school matron. That is until the day puberty began to announce itself down below. She clocked my short-and-curlies, smirked and left. I just sat in the bathroom and cried at the humiliation and embarrassment of it all. And she never came in again after that.'

Max punched the pillow. 'I think a son's love started to die that day.'

'Oh dear!'

'She has to be in control. She has to know every tiny thing that's going on around her so she can use it for her own ends. It's mean-spirited and corrosive.'

'Poor Max,' said Zena, rubbing the back of his neck. 'I always thought it wuz sad when she stopped you playin' with us village kids . . .'

'And, don't forget, removed me from the village school! How old was I? Five or six? I loved going to school across the road. Had all sorts of mates. Played football and cricket with all of them. Even Bostock. If anything, he was my best pal! Then suddenly I'm hooked out and sent to "a school more befitting a young gentleman." Overnight I became the stuck-up boy at the big house too bloody good to be allowed to mix with the hoi-polloi. How unjust was that?'

Zena recognized the truth of what he had said and nuzzled his neck.

'I can still hear them having a blazing row about it in the library.'

'Your father was opposed to it?'

'Sounded like it. I couldn't hear very clearly but he was on the defensive. She was wading into him. About how I needed better influences in my life. He was clearly setting a bad example . . . things like that. Sounded vicious and, thinking of it now, highly personal stuff, designed to cut deep. A man with any gumption would have socked her!'

'Max!' she chided. 'Violence is no answer! You should know that b'now!'

He nodded apologetically. 'Well, he might at least have shown some backbone and walked out on the woman. Frankly, I've no idea how the marriage has survived.'

'Could it be love?' she said with a mannered wobble of the head.

Max blew a raspberry. 'Fat chance! I couldn't hear much of what he said in response but he must have caved in, like he does on everything else. My father's made of putty as far as she's concerned. He just looks the other way when she applies the pressure or stands there looking as vacant as a scarecrow.'

'I always thought he wuz a kind man . . .'

'He is, but kindness is no good if you want to survive against my mother! You must give as good as you get. That means giving no quarter . . . bearing grudges and settling them! My Old Man hasn't got the balls to tell her when she's talking twaddle. He let himself down. He let us both down. Damn it, he let me down!'

'You makes your mother sound a schemin' bitch!'

Max grimaced. 'I think you've got the message. She's always scheming. Her next wheeze is to marry me off to blasted Vanessa Devereux!'

Zena felt a hot flush drench her body, forcing her to hold him tighter.

'That Devereux creature has been the bane of my life. Ever since the day she was brought round to the house as a suitable playmate. I ask you, I was a six-year-old boy! What kind of playmate was that! The precious boy at the big house has to play with girls!'

He smoothed out the pillow. 'So that's my parents for you. Never a caring word or touch for their own sake. Quick to chide and slow to praise. Emotions always hidden away—which is what made that row so memorable. The trick is to pretend everything is fine and dandy on the surface. Anything festering underneath is to be overlooked. Learn to cope on your own. So I did. I became emotionally self-reliant. Not altogether a bad thing. I learnt what it was like to stand alone. I built a protective wall around myself, keeping my resentment at this lack of a storybook family inside and keeping everyone else outside. But the resentment developed into a bitterness the size of a giant boil that I grew incapable of lancing. It poisoned my emotions. It triggered a physical detachment. Solitude became my best friend. I preferred my own company, marched to the beat of my own drum, happy to be regarded a maverick, someone best avoided. Gradually came to prefer animals to people!'

'Does that include me?'

'No,' he said, stroking her face. 'How could you imagine such a thing. What would I do without you—or daft Chick.'

Zena lifted her head from his hand.

'But you're special,' he added quickly. 'Always have been. Always will be. No one could ever take your place.'

'Good,' she said, nestling her head back down again. 'I'm glad.'

'But at least you know where you are with animals!' he added.

Max shook his head and laughed: Zena's bed was an unlikely confessional box and she an improbable confessor. But it was making him feel better.

'I've never heard you talk loik this . . .'

'It's the trenches talking. This war loosens the tongue.'

'Then get it all off your chest. I don't moind.'

He thought for a moment. 'Well, that wall was cemented by anger so pathological I became fearful of it being released. So I turned it inward and became a slave to melancholy. It seemed to me the safer option.'

Zena tried to look into his eyes to see if he was telling the absolute truth but he turned his head away again.

'Keeping up appearances, that's all it's been about,' he added with a sigh. 'All three of us. Me. My mother. And my father. Doing it for the sake of the family. Yet there is no family. Lawn Upton's like the bloody Marie Celeste! From a distance people might be fooled into thinking everything's normal but once you get on board and look inside there's no sign of a damned crew!'

She hugged him and kissed the top of his head.

'We're just three people who don't appear to get on with each other. Three vessels sailing around the same sea without ever hailing each other.'

'I waunts to 'elp, if I could. You knows that . . .'

'Even Freud would scratch his head faced with the Lanhams!'

'. . . but fam'ly is fam'ly . . .'

'Yes, it's unfair of me to saddle you with all this. You'll have to stop being such a good listener!'

'Max,' she said, 'why don't you just leave home. You'll destroy yourself if you carry on loik this. You has the money to rent some rooms of your own in the town.'

Max pressed his head into the pillow. 'I've asked myself that question over and over. And what stops me? Duty . . . loyalty . . .'

Max tipped his head back and smiled. 'And do you know what? Those are the principles my mother hammered into me. That's her legacy.'

'So, she gave you summut worthwhile . . .'

'Yes,' he conceded. 'And it's the same set of grand ideals they drummed into me at school. Things one should aspire to. Things that matter. Things that are worth fighting for. Your family . . . good causes.'

Max gestured toward the chair in the corner. 'The things that put me in that uniform over there.'

'En't there anyone else you can talk to?' Zena said, burrowing under the bedclothes. 'Help you get your moind sorted . . .'

'I don't want to bleed all over people if I can help it.'

'No relatives?'

'No. My father had one brother. But he died from lock-jaw as a boy after cutting his hand on a broken beer bottle. My grandmother Jacobson is still alive. But she never visits any more. She's 70-something now and too infirm. Still lives in the same old cottage at the top end of Hollow Way she was born in.'

'Then visit her . . .'

'I do, when I can,' he said trying to disguise the guilt in his voice for it was several years since he had done so. 'Her mind's still as sharp as a tack. She's a bit rough round the edges. Always dunked her toast in her tea even when she had teeth! Came from a large family of farm labourers. Her daughter married well, you might say. But she's a good old stick and a good listener. I was thinking of going up to see her in a couple of days. Before I return to France. Seize a final opportunity, as it were . . .'

'Don't talk loik that!'

'Granny Jake might be some help, I suppose,' Max replied defensively.

Zena's face suddenly brightened. 'An' what about that old schoolmaster of yours you loiked so much?'

'Now, that is a thought.'

Max snuggled down beside her. 'You're right. I should release my demons. Or I may just go off my head . . . and then you'll be visiting me in that loony bin down the road!'

'Stop it, Max!' she said, clipping his ear playfully.

'I must go to Iffley in any case. Got to do a favour for someone. Shouldn't waste the opportunity. I'll pop in on Ben Newsam at the same time.'

8

Iffley

Max woke again at first light, his body programmed to 'stand-to' just like any other morning. The sunlight was already stretching across the ceiling and he could hear the bees buzzing in the hollyhocks below the window.

He swung his legs out from under the sheet, and then could not resist lifting it to take one last peep at Zena, huddled up into a soft pink ball like some hibernating dormouse. He scrambled into his clothes, then stooped to plant one final kiss on her forehead. She sighed and rolled languidly onto her back. He relived the softness of her breasts, the curve of her hips, the moistness of her lips, and blew a dry whistle. It was all he could do to leave.

But his brain was consumed by the smell of the bacon he knew to be frying on Mrs Tedder's range, and fantasized about the golden-yolked eggs soon to make its acquaintance on the plate. He sneaked through Lawn Upton's kitchen door and dug his fingertips into the cook's well upholstered ribs, causing her to take a firm grip of her frying pan. She roundly scolded him for 'creepin' up on an old woman loik that! You'll be the death o' me!' But her admonishment came with a kindly skin-cracking smile that reduced her flat round face to something resembling a well baked ginger biscuit.

Observing Mrs Tedder in her domain, strands of silvery hair escaping from beneath her skewed hat, her checked pinny scraping the floor, brought back delicious memories: of wet afternoons sitting at the end of the table, head propped on elbows, sizing up the generous dollops of cake mix round the sides of the bowl which, once pushed his way, he might scoop up with his fingers.

Or of making an actual sighting of Doll Tedder's husband, Fred. The Tedders had worked for the Lanham family all their lives, she in the kitchen, he in the garden. Fred was as skeletal as she was stout, and sightings of him were as rare as Banquo's ghost for he moved around his own fiefdom as stealthily as she navigated hers like a top-heavy galleon under full sail. For years Doll (short for Dorothy) used Fred as a 'bogeyman', convincing the young Max that her husband was nothing more than a figment of everyone's imagination: only a rustling in the herbaceous border or a smoking pile of refuse or a freshly pruned bed of roses betraying his presence. When Max finally sat next to the old man one tea-time, inhaling the strange pong of tobacco, ale and compost, an enduring friendship was initiated with a knowing wink and sealed by a finger tapped against his bulb of a nose.

Max parked himself at the thick-topped table beside the initials ML he'd carved back in 1905 that drew a fearful ticking-off and clipped ear from Mrs Tedder. One look at his 'little-boy face', as she called it, told her he couldn't wait to eat his breakfast 'in the proper place, loik a gentleman, loik his father.' Fred Tedder read his wife's glance: he'd have to wait for his breakfast a while longer. The needs of Master Max came first. He sucked on his pipe and smiled. A wife denied children by some act known only to God had been given back the nearest to it.

Max watched Mrs Tedder glide around the kitchen as if on familiar rails, finally halting to fork two rashers of bacon onto a plate from a serving dish she extracted from the warming oven—adding two more as he tut-tutted twice—and then flipping an egg alongside them.

'You'll aff to wait for 'nother egg,' she said in an Ox accent thicker than Zena's, though not so impenetrable as Granny Jake's. 'I s'pose you'll want one, you greedy beggar. And you can sloice an' butter your own bread!'

Max studied what he knew to be the tastiest bacon and eggs this side of breakfast heaven for a split second, and then wolfed them down as if this was the first meal he had eaten in months. Mrs Tedder reached up to the top left-hand hook on the welsh dresser and brought down the blue tin mug. She filled it three-quarters full with tea, topped it up with milk and dropped in three heaped teaspoonfuls of sugar.

'There, just as you loiks it, Master Max,' she said, running a hand heavy with the scent of bacon grease along Max's shoulder, which ensured every forkful he swallowed tasted all the porkier. She looked toward her husband and mouthed something not intended for Max's ears, the whispered code of the long married, one perfected by decades of fireside conversation. Fred Tedder gave his pipe another suck and nodded.

Max mopped his plate with his remaining scrap of bread, downed the last of his tea and planted an exaggerated kiss on Mrs Tedder's cheek. The he crept upstairs to his room, where he bathed and shaved. After brushing and donning uniform and boots, he went back down through the kitchen and took the path that skirted the churchyard and vicarage garden; he crossed the lane and cut down Longwall to meet the Oxford road opposite Adelaide House, the iron-railinged home of the Kempsons. From there it was a pleasant amble up and over Rose Hill to Iffley.

It would have offered a pleasant amble had his state of mind been in any other condition than its present one. The more he walked the more he wanted to abort the journey, his pledge to a fellow officer notwithstanding. There was no telling what social disasters that would lead to. And if he knew Ben Newsam every bit as much as he thought he did there was every chance he might be sent packing with a flea in his ear. Cresting the top of the hill he paused to remove his cap and mop the sweaty red strip where the brow-band had rubbed. He'd no choice but to go on.

Thee sun was climbing high in the June sky by the time he passed beneath the squat tower of Iffley's Norman church that attracted visitors from all over the country to view the elaborate Romanesque carvings decorating its doorways. Ben Newsam's whitewashed cottage, the venue for many a six-form debate, garden party or career discussion, was a little farther down Church Way, the end one of three lying under a long blue slate roof on the corner of Mill Lane.

Through the jungle of amorous lupins and foxgloves, Max spied his mentor crouched over the rockery by the door and was about to call out when the figure stood up. Max stopped. It was too scruffy to be Ben Newsam. And on the cottage wall Max could plainly see what

71

the interloper had been up to: he'd got as far as scrawling 'YELLER CONCHEE BAST . . .'

Max broke into a run, yelling as he went. The unwelcome visitor instantly hurdled the stone wall and sprinted down Mill Lane in the direction of the river. But Max had seen enough to put a name to him.

'Max, is that you making all that racket down there?'

At the dormer window above the front door was the pale face of Ben Newsam. 'Wait there, I'll be straight down.'

Newsam opened the door and his dark eyes followed Max's to what had been daubed on the wall. 'I see . . .'

'I saw who it was,' said Max.

'There's plenty to choose from!' said Newsam, rubbing at the 'Y' with his handkerchief so the lock of black hair that flopped over his left eye jumped up and down. 'No . . . really?'

Max stood hands on hips, shaking his head. 'Well, the head of hair alone gave this one away. There's only one ginger nut around here nowadays . . .'

'Ah, Eddie Bostock!'

'. . . who can't spell,' continued Max. 'Here, let me help.'

'It's no use, Max. This charcoal is the devil to remove. Just smudges. Best to cover it.'

'Oi! Come on! Join in!'

They looked across the street to see Eddie Bostock conducting an invisible choir.

Send out the Ar-mee an' the Nay-vee!
Send out the rank an' file.
Send out me brother, me sister an' me mother,
But fer Gawd's sake don't send me!

Bostock stopped singing along to his imaginary baton and ran off, whooping.

Max made to pursue him, but Newsam pulled him back and led him round to the outhouse.

'Not the first time this has happened, then?' Max said, spotting two empty cans of whitewash on the floor beside the mangle.

Newsam's mouth broke into that knowing smile he used to allow himself whenever one of the Oxbridge class stated the obvious—or actually humoured him. Max loved to tease it from him and regarded its appearance as an accolade: it did not really qualify as a smile, thought Max, more of a desultory nod in the direction of amusement. Like the day sweating over Latin grammar when Newsam asked what case should Cassivilaunus be in if Caesar killed him and instead of answering 'Accusative, sir' he had volunteered 'Coffin, sir!'

Newsam was never a joke-cracking master, leaving that to his pupils. Yet no one took liberties in his classes: intelligent sixth-formers, which by definition they were, recognize instinctively when they are playing headstrong Alexander to wise Aristotle. The basis of Newsam's teaching was conversation, discussion, argument—reasoned and civilized, not a shouting match—which might take place anywhere at any time. The favoured few were taken to the Ashmolean and regaled with stories of the museum's relics that no ordinary guide would relate: Guy Fawkes's lantern led to the goriest tales of the Gunpowder Plotter's torture and execution; King Alfred's Jewel to the recipe for Saxon oat-cakes.

Compared to the rest of the 'beaks' at Magdalen College School, Newsam was not so much unorthodox as heretical. He was also of a different generation, coming across more like an elder brother than a father or an uncle: he patrolled the corridors with the strut of a man comfortable in his own skin, a man reluctant to compromise—just the kind of man a sixth former deferred to. And he was no mean sport, cutting a splendid dash with a rugby ball or a cricket bat in his hands. Slight he may have been, but if he scythed you down, his bony shoulder impaling soft belly, you knew you had been tackled; and any return catch off his bat in the nets resulted in a stinging hand-shaker for the bowler. Finally, there was that intriguing squiggle of a scar on his left cheekbone, the so-called 'duelling scar' according to prefect-room gossip. That it turned out to be the result of the infant Newsam running into the corner of a table was never allowed to ruin the man's mystique.

'Here, let me,' said Max, peeling off his jacket and reaching for a paintbrush.

Newsam feigned horror. 'Certainly not! And dirty the King's uniform! No, you may fetch the beer—you know where it is, don't you? And then you may mount guard in the event our young patriot

73

returns to gloat. Probably thought you'd come to haul me off in chains to the nearest internment camp!'

Max left Newsam to his painting and fetched two bottles of Morrell's pale ale from the stone cold-store in the corner of the scullery; he thumbed up the stoppers and passed one to Newsam. They clinked bottles and sat down on the front doorstep to drink. With each swig their expressions grew more serious.

Newsam was first to break the silence. 'So, Max, excuse my bluntness but what is it that you want to talk about? Something's worrying you or you wouldn't waste precious leave visiting the likes of me!'

The bottle hovered at Max's lips, though not from the cause of his visit being questioned. 'You can't think I agree with the Bostocks of this world?'

'I couldn't—wouldn't—blame you if you did.'

'Sir, you've always been a man of principle,' Max countered, clenching his fist. 'We all applauded that at MCS. There was that time you took on the Head over . . .'

Newsam raised his bottle. 'Max, opposing one's Headmaster over plans to double the CCF budget is one thing, refusing to fight for one's country quite another.'

'But you're too old!' protested Max. 'Too unfit!'

Newsam sighed at his former pupil's half-hearted smokescreen. 'Not now. I'm right on the mark now conscription has risen to 40. And they say it'll go up again to 50 if things don't improve. As for fitness, they're so desperate I'd be rated A1 these days.'

'I wasn't aware.'

'Do you know how many men have been registered as conscientious objectors since the Military Services Act was put into practice 15 months ago?'

Max looked at the ground.

'Something like fifteen thousand. They even locked up Bertrand Russell for speaking out against the war. And how many men have been killed in this conflict so far?'

Max nodded. 'We lost 150,000 men in this recent push at Arras.'

'You see? A paltry few thousand COs are not worth bothering about by comparison. What's the fuss? Pack the conchies off to work camps on Dartmoor, digging ditches or some other fruitless exercise. It makes not one happorth of difference why a man refuses to fight, refuses to countenance killing his fellow man. Refusal to swear the oath is sufficient to brand him with the mark of a coward.'

'Sir, you're no coward!'

'Try telling that to Bostock and his fellow daubers or those who send me white feathers! A volunteer army was one thing but since conscription either you accept the call-up and do your duty or you don't.'

'Why not . . .'

'Max, let me tell you something I've never told a living soul.'

Newsam had turned to prop himself on outstretched arms against the wall. Head down, he began to speak in a halting voice as if racked with guilt.

'When I was a young boy my father gave me a rifle and taught me how to use it. In time, he suggested I practice for the real thing, by which he meant for war, by shooting the birds that came to nest in our garden. Shooting one of those unsuspecting and harmless blackbirds proved all too straightforward. But as it lay there on the lawn, quite motionless, its mate flew down from a tree and began circling the dead bird, jumping and squawking, imploring it to get up and fly away. One bird suffered death. The other suffered in life. Death and living death. I'd caused all that suffering. By using a gun. And I vowed never to cause it again.'

Max was grateful he couldn't see Newsam's face. That way they'd both avoided embarrassment. Newsam tilted his bottle high to obtain its last dregs.

'Agree to join the Non Combatant Corps . . .'

'Ah,' sneered Newsam, 'what they call "The No Courage Corps"!'

His black eyes were now in Max's face. 'Look Max, I'll not play any part in this war—even digging ditches with the NCC. This war, like every one before it, will be ended by people who lifted not one finger in anger throughout the duration sitting down round a table and talking. Why not sit down and talk before they slaughter hundreds of thousands of each other?'

Max started to form a reply but knew he had no answer worth articulating: nobody ever tried more than once to impose a worthless argument on Ben Newsam.

'I'll not contribute to this war effort in any shape or form,' Newsam emphasized with a sweep of his hand. 'And I shall inform the local tribunal as such. That puts me among the 1,500 or so die-hards they're calling "absolutists" so there'll be no possibility of exemption being granted. I'll be tried and bound for some kind of incarceration.'

'Who's on the tribunal?'

'Assorted local dignitaries . . . middle-class patriots like Tinegate from your parish council and ex-Army buffers like old Amor!'

Max swatted a fly, and shook his head sorrowfully.

'So I'll not even bother to apply.'

'Won't the school stick up for you?'

'I was coming to that! The governors met three weeks ago and by eight votes to two voted to remove me from my post. Hardly a surprise in the circumstances. The school has already contributed 204 sixth formers for commissions besides your good self, plus nine masters.'

Max was reduced to feeling as empty and useless as the beer bottle he was holding

That's enough about the bed I've made for myself,' said Newsam, placing his own bottle on the doorstep. 'Now, what is it that's on your mind?'

A coldness enveloped Max as Newsam's question stirred up the same old images. He sucked in some air and blew out a few staccato sentences describing the events of 9 May. By the time he ran out of words he could feel his arm shaking.

'So, you see, the first man I've knowingly killed in this war was one of my own.'

Newsam patted Max's wrist and felt the radial vein pumping against his fingertips.

'I believe my nerves have gone,' croaked Max. 'Before the execution I pretty much coped, no nerves of steel but I managed to blot things out of my mind. Now for no accountable reason I shiver and tremble with unknown fear. On my last night op before coming home I was out with a wiring party repairing the wire and I stood holding a spade, petrified and shaking. I wanted to return to the dugout but couldn't let the men down. In the blackness of the night all the fears came crowding in. I was in the grip of an unreasoning terror that made me want to go screaming, anywhere, to get away from the noise of the guns, the horror, the filth and the lice. But there was no escape. Go forward onto the wire and I'd as likely be shot. Go back to the support trenches and Johnny Redcap would soon be hunting me. Then there'd be a court martial by men—chateau generals we call them—who could never know what it was like to be afraid of waking each day and wondering whether it would be your last. Men who would order a man—no a boy—to be shot for desertion or cowardice. I know. I saw it happen. I pulled the trigger. I had that boy's brains all over me.'

Newsam held Max's wrist in silence, searching for words to express his compassion but finding only a mouth as dry as the Kalahari.

'Sir, I tell you this,' said Max looking Newsam in the eye. 'No man who has served in the trenches should ever be called a coward.'

'I couldn't agree more.'

Max bit his lip and concentrated on a stray cloud, weighing up what he wanted to say.

'I don't think I can go back. I feel so . . . alone. I no more fit-in there than I do here. I can never be just one of the men and I despise the officer class, brave though most of them are. I've nowhere to call home. The trenches have sucked me dry . . . shattered my nerves . . . eventually they'll have my body.'

'Max, stop chasing the mice in your skull!,' said Newsam, tightening his grip on Max's wrist. 'I'm no man to tell you whether to fight but desertion is not an option for you . . .'

Max recognized the sadness in Newsam's jet-black eyes. 'I'm sorry, sir. Why am I being so dense? If anyone knows about isolation it's you.'

Newsam did not bother to nod.

'I thought I might make a run for Ireland,' Max continued. 'Things are wild out there at present. Plenty of places for a man to hide. Could take a boat to America from there . . .'

'So you've given it that amount of thought?' Newsam observed with a shrug.

'Why don't we both go?' Max had made the suggestion before he knew just how desperate it made him sound. Yet desperate was exactly how he felt.

'Running away is no solution to any problem, Max. How often have I told you that.'

The heat in Max's cheeks faded under this splash of cold logic.

Newsam continued to employ the stern expression of mentor, confessor and surrogate father. 'What about your family? Think how this would affect them? It would destroy them.'

Max tipped his head back and laughed. 'My family? What family? We're three people who happen to share the same name and the same house. To my mother I'm something to parade—preferably in uniform—before people she calls friends but in reality are no more than chisellers and cheap opportunists. To my father . . .'

'He was always so proud of you,' Newsam interjected. 'Seldom did I see a prouder parent on the touchline at school matches than your father.'

Max mouth fell open. 'Pity he never expressed an opinion on my game, or come to that, ever told me he was there!'

'In point of fact, he and I discussed that very thing one Saturday afternoon and he replied he didn't want to risk putting you off your game by telling you he was going to watch.'

'There, see what I mean?' spluttered Max. 'There's no communication in our family! My father will happily sit shuffling in his armchair, staring blankly, willing me to conduct both sides of a conversation, provide answers to my own questions and read his thoughts to avoid the strain of expressing them himself.'

'He used to be a fair player himself, you know. I saw him turn out at fly-half for Town versus Gown at Iffley Road one year.'

'You see!' exclaimed Max, thumping palms to temples. 'I never knew that. Just think of the advice he could pass on if he had a mind.'

'Then perhaps you should take the responsibility and ask him.'

'I tell myself that, I really do. But, damn it, he is my father. He's the head of the family and should take responsibility, whether he likes it or not.'

'There's more to it than . . .'

Max wasn't listening. 'Do you know, he's never once physically chastised me.'

'Nothing wrong with that. The belt is no cure . . .'

'I tend to think it would have done our relationship a power of good had he administered a stroke or two. I've certainly given him plenty of excuses. I'd have respected him far more had he taken the slipper to me when I disrespected him. But he didn't. And so we Lanhams just dodder on, existing in our individual boxes! Freud would need a decade to sort us out!'

'If there was some way I could help, I would gladly . . .'

'You are, sir,' Max said softly. 'You're listening. I must talk to someone or I fear I'll lose my mind completely. And then it'll be sticking my head above the parapet during a full moon and let a Boche sniper take care of the problem for me.'

Newsam stood up, his lips white with the shock of listening to the son he never had spout such irresponsible nonsense. 'Don't talk like that Max! Never wish your life away, not on any account. You were not taught to treat life, or yourself, so lightly.'

Max ran his hands back through his hair, feeling as though Newsam had awarded him yet another Sunday morning detention for insolence. Why, he asked himself, was he plagued by this destructive knack of lashing out and hurting those precious few people he loved? Why was there only black and white on his emotional palette?

'Sir, please take care,' he said, offering his hand. 'But stick to your principles.'

Newsam took his hand and grasped his elbow. 'You, too, Max. God be with you.'

'By the way,' said Max absent mindedly, 'do you know the precise whereabouts of Nowell House?'

Some lightness returned to Newsam's voice. 'The Beenham's place? Fifty yards down the road, on the right. The old school.'

'Ah, yes, I know it.' said Max. 'Do you recall Peter Revell? Tallish chap, horsey face. Good cricketer, kept wicket.'

'Of course,' said Newsam, wagging a finger. 'Left early. Wanted to enter the service.'

'Well, he did that all right. Picked up a Special Reserve commission. He's a captain in my battalion. He's asked me to look in on his fiancée. See how she is and what not. Bit of a bugbear to tell the truth but he'd do the same for me, I'm sure.'

'I didn't realize the Beenhams had a daughter . . .'

'They haven't!' cut in Max. 'She's the children's governess. Name of Hawes, Rowan Hawes.'

9

Long Bridges

In just a matter of seconds Max was pulling the bell-rope at Nowell House. He announced himself to the maid and was shown into the sitting room.

He heard the sound of a piano coming from another room and shut his eyes the better to hear its tinkling wagtail runs and thumping chords. The music, and the mood, was suddenly curtailed, and he opened his eyes just in time to see Rowan Hawes enter—though she didn't so much enter the room as bound into it in the manner of a young red setter chasing gulls on a beach.

She had been dreading this moment as much as her visitor, and hoped her bravado would not be interpreted as over-confidence. 'It's so good of you to call,' she said behind a smile and an extended hand. 'Peter wrote me. How is he . . . and how are you?'

Max took gentle hold of her hand: an hour-old fawn could not have trembled more. He sensed her embarrassment at being placed in this awkward situation, touching upon emotive subjects with a complete stranger. He told her everything Revell had instructed him to say and lied in answer to questions where the truth was better left unsaid. In response, he learnt that she came from a small town in Bedfordshire where her parents ran a greengrocery; had come to Oxford to train as a teacher; and had met Revell at a dance in the Town Hall. His first impression was of a homely young woman rather than a hungry careerist: yes, that was it, he decided, the dutiful kind of woman who would make a first-class wife and mother.

Courteously, and wisely, he kept his wildly chauvinistic impressions to himself. Otherwise his acquaintance with Rowan Hawes would have been severed by a fiery glare and an even hotter turn of phrase. As it was, she quickly found herself disconcerted by the notion that he was looking right through her and examining the wallpaper: she fancied he might, had he chose, even have identified any false joins in the pattern.

'So, I gather you and Peter are to be married?' Max continued in a voice sporting a fair amount of bounce of its own. But in his case, entirely false.

'Yes, that's correct. And then Peter would like to try one of the dominions, Australia or Canada perhaps. Once this war is over!'

Max smiled and looked at his wristwatch. 'I must be making a move.'

She'd detected the slight grimace and sensed the real cause of his discomfort. She was feeling the same: sitting on egg-shells wondering how to carry on a civil conversation without mentioning the dreaded 'w' word.

'I suppose you must get heartily sick of people saying . . .'

'. . . once the war is over?'

'I'm sorry,' she said, dropping her eyes. 'It was tactless and inexcusably insensitive of me. You're on leave. Absolutely the last thing you want to hear mentioned is the war.'

'Unavoidable, I'm afraid.' He looked up and thought he saw tears in her eyes.

'It is I who should be apologizing,' he said. 'I'm here to re-assure you and I've managed to upset you instead.'

'Take no notice,' she said dabbing her eyes, her voice starting to break.

Her worst fears had been realized: she was behaving like a convent girl in a hot funk at being made to converse with a boy from the school over the hill. She had her reasons: aside from Mr Beenham, she had had hardly any social contact with a man outside her family since Peter went to France a year ago. But it annoyed her that she could be so skittish.

She cleared her throat with a controlled cough. 'I'm stronger than you think . . . stronger than I look.'

Max had no idea why he did it, either at the time or subsequently whenever the moment crossed his mind, but he suddenly heard himself exuding a charm he never knew he possessed.

'Well, let's put you to the test!' he said. 'How about we take a walk along the river? It's a beautiful day, far too good to waste sitting indoors moping. We could walk into town—if you feel energetic. Take tea at the Clarendon if you like . . .'

Her eyes brightened, not, Max hoped, with more tears. 'No, you mustn't put yourself out like that. I'm being quite pathetic . . .'

'I'll take that as a yes!'

Gradually, as if pulled by invisible strings, her mouth widened into a crinkly smile which slowly travelled to her pale green eyes and transformed them into what Max immediately likened to some shimmering rock pools that once entranced him with the promise of sunken treasure during a summer holiday in Criccieth.

'You're so kind . . . I'd love to, she said, getting to her feet and brushing out the folds of her satin skirt. 'I'll just change into something more suitable for walking if I may?'

She poured Max a glass of Rose's lime cordial and left him sifting through the magazines. He pushed aside the current issue of *The Lady*, and settled back on the sofa thumbing through *Horse & Hound* until a cloud of scent he identified as jasmine-based announced her return. She had changed into a long high-waisted dress of white cotton piped in blue that paid tribute to her curves and displayed the merest hint of a shapely stockinged ankle above a pair of neat, but sturdy, white boots. Only an emerald heart-shaped broach remained from before.

'There! Will I do?' she smiled, unconvincingly in her view.

Max smiled back, dutifully he hoped.

He waited for her to pick up her parasol from the hat-stand and opened the front door for her. They crossed the road and set off down Mill Lane with the stiff gait of two self-conscious penguins, each of them drawing in their tummy muscles and lifting heads high as if their ears were magnetized from above.

They paid their halfpenny toll to the old woman at the booth and followed the meandering path which led through the shade of the nearby stand of poplar trees and past the mill, reduced to a blackened shell following the disastrous fire of 1908, until they crossed the weir and reached the lock. One of Salters saloon steamers on the downstream run to Henley was in the process of being dropped foot by foot through the lock so they took a position on the adjacent stone bridge villagers referred to as the Roving Bridge to enjoy a better vantage point.

Max began to wonder what he had let himself in for. It was his own silly fault: he had never considered himself prone to chivalrous acts and this uncharacteristic aberration explained why. He leant over the balustrade and the sight of a hawthorn twig floating by caused his mind to wander: 'I dropped the berry in the stream . . .'

'. . . and caught a little silver trout . . . 'she responded.

'The silver apples of the moon . . . 'he continued.

'. . . The golden apples of the sun,' she replied.

Max felt his face giving birth to a smile but tried not to appear too enthusiastic. 'You like Yeats?'

'Oh, yes! I must confess to preferring Byron but Yeats is growing on me,' she replied exultantly, relieved to have stumbled upon some common ground. 'You too?'

Max was cheered by the zest in her voice. Thus far it had seemed in keeping with its owner's occupation: the occasionally jolly, but prone to being assertive, tone of the governess. Now both properties were usurped by a breathless delivery bordering on huskiness which Max found seductive.

'We soldiers are not all philistines, you know!' he said, pulling a face.

Her hand went to her open mouth and she heard Revell's voice saying something similar in his own defence.

'Oh, I'm so sorry! So rude of me . . . I shouldn't tar all soldiers with the same brush. I just thought poetry was less of, how can I put it, a "manly" interest.'

'I must confess to loving nothing better than a good Henty adventure story as a boy but I've enough adventure in my life these days!'

She could feel herself cringing with embarrassment at this latest gaffe and wondered whether it might be best if she feigned a headache and asked to be taken home.

'Poetry makes you—or at least me—think about its meaning, makes me concentrate more on its meaning than a novel; it encourages us to explore our emotions, let the soul escape for a bit—no bad thing for a soldier, I can assure you!.'

'Of course. I understand.'

'As for Yeats, one of my masters at Magdalen College School—one of your neighbours, actually—introduced me to his work.'

'His verse is so spare, raw yet so beautiful, so heart-felt, positively ethereal,' she said in a voice rising with renewed enthusiasm. 'His words sit there on the page aching.'

'Do you know why?'

'His muse, you mean? Maud Gonne?' she ventured. 'The unrequited love of his life—and many others besides, I believe.'

Max watched the sunlight playing with her fine hair, teasing it into a pale bronze mass of spun sugar that drifted on the breeze like a comet's tail. She wore it shoulder-length, with just enough clearance, he now noticed, for it to swing back and forth freely whenever her conversation grew animated.

'I wonder why she never married him?'

'He certainly asked her enough times . . .'

'Again this year, I read,' she said. 'And when she rejected him yet again he proposed to her daughter!'

'Is that so?'

'Yes, and she, too, spurned him! Isn't that tragic? Now the gossip columns are saying he's proposed to . . .'

'But, just think,' said Max, 'had she married him the muse may have left him and we'd not have eight exquisitely crafted lines like those of . . .'

'He wishes for the clothes of gold?'

Max nodded and they recited the last line in unison: 'Tread softly, because you tread on my dreams.'

She looked into the distance, briefly transported by Yeats to the land of her own dreams, one peopled by Revell, her children and her animals. Then she remembered where she was and who she was with.

'If the photographs do her any justice at all,' she said, tapping the balustrade with her parasol, 'I can appreciate why Yeats was so besotted with her.'

'An Amazon with honey-gold hair, hazel eyes and a complexion like the blossom of apples,' drooled Max with a soppy schoolboy grin. 'Or so I've read!'

'You're smitten too!' she replied, her voice dipping and rising on each syllable.

'And intelligent with it!' he added behind the makings of a blush. 'The first woman to muscle in on the Dublin literary circle.'

'And such a firebrand! If she were the Nationalist leader Ireland would have won Home Rule by now!'

'Yes, the Irish Joan of Arc, they say. Her police file must be three inches thick by now. Beautiful, clever and feisty! Quite a lethal combination!'

A grin began to fill out her cheeks, causing her big green eyes to screw up behind tiny crows feet. Emboldened, she edged closer and engaged him face to face. 'Come on! Admit it! You've quite a crush on her?'

He felt challenged, not so much by her question as her proximity. The warmth of her naked skin at wrist and neck intensified the intoxicating aroma of her scent and made him feel quite giddy. Zena smelt earthy, feral, like some woodland creature and made him feel equally wild with the desire to possess her. This scent was understated, purer; it was not trying to send any message but in so trying only succeeded in transmitting a stronger one. It communicated the very essence of Rowan Hawes: it was demure yet captivating, unassuming yet confident. And it was hypnotic. He was beginning to feel envious of Peter Revell.

'If one was fortunate enough to meet anyone so alluring,' he found himself saying, 'he might count himself a very lucky man indeed.'

For the first time Max dared to look her directly in the face. It was a round face with full cheeks and a small strong nose bedecked with freckles whose presence suggested her flawless complexion responded eagerly to summer sun. Her lips were as ripe as her cheeks and her mouth seemed set in a permanent half-smile. And then there were her green eyes: huge, beguiling and expressive orbs, capable of probing like searchlights one minute or scintillating like emeralds the next as if they were fired by some powerful electric charge.

Now her freckles darkened and she avoided his gaze lest she be forced to acknowledge the embarrassment she was sure she must be causing him.

Max touched her elbow. 'Shall we walk on?'

They decided against halting for a drink at The Isis Hotel: instead Max bought a bar of chocolate from the machine beside the towpath to sustain them and lightened the mood by insisting they test the strength of the penny weighing contraption alongside it—only to discover the needle whizzed round the dial with no inclination to stop.

They sauntered onward, debating whether Maud Gonne should have married Yeats instead of the soldier-patriot Sean McBride. As she grew more comfortable in Max's company she continually stole a half-step on him, like an impatient puppy eager to play, and even took to walking backwards if it made eye contact easier. Max found himself relaxing, talking without thinking, lulled by her ability to listen and convey an interest in what he had to say.

They lost track of time but after some twenty minutes or so they reached Long Bridges, a loop in the river bounded by trees that had been converted into a safe area for bathing. Their attention was diverted by the sound of two boys rampaging through a clump of trees, waving sticks and whooping like Zulus: one of the boys was Eddie Bostock.

'Hey, sol-jer boy, come an' look at this!'

'Yeh, come on!' echoed his disciple.

'Or are yer too yeller?'

After this morning's episode, Max was in the mood to cuff Bostock round the ear there and then, that is until he felt an arm entwine itself with his.

'What mischief have you got up to now?' he said instead.

The boys led them into the trees. 'There! Look!'

Max went the final yards alone and there on the ground was a half-grown rabbit, nose twitching pathetically, its body stretched and limp. He went down on one knee to examine it and saw it had a jagged bite mark to the throat and was clearly close to death.

'Yer can't leave it loik that, sol-jer boy!' shouted Bostock.

'Yer'll 'ave to kill it!' said the younger boy, jumping up and down.

'Go on! Kill it! I dares yer!' challenged Bostock, shaking his stick.

Max took the stick from him and one look at the bloodied point confirmed his suspicion. 'You've been torturing the poor thing haven't you?'

'We wuz just seein' if it were dead, thass all.'

'You nasty little toe-rag!' hissed Max. 'Haven't you got up to enough mischief today already? Get out of here before I lay this stick across your backside!'

The young Bostock retreated a safe distance. 'You do an' I'll 'ave me dad on yer. An' me brother.'

'And I shall take this stick to the pair of them!' said a female voice firmly.

Rowan Hawes had caught up, and had heard quite enough. She tried to breathe slowly and deeply to calm down but failed lamentably: she snatched the stick from Max's grasp and snapped it in half, routing the boys as if they were Betsy Trotwood's donkeys.

They were right, of course, thought Max: the rabbit ought to be put out of its misery. But he would rather have let nature take its course than appearing to act so callously in front of a lady. He stood for a moment as if he were waiting for the whistle to blow, wondering what she was thinking but knowing she could not be asked. Then he picked up the rabbit by its hind legs, went behind the nearest tree and dispatched it by smacking its head against the trunk just like Fred Tedder had taught him. He prayed that she had not witnessed the gory scene.

She had not. She had wandered ahead and he found her on one of the bridges crossing the loop, sheltering beneath her parasol from the burning afternoon sun. Her first thought, as he suspected, was to distance herself from the event for she had no wish to see an animal suffering. Her second thought he had no reason to suspect: she had no wish to see him suffering.

She heard his footsteps click-clacking across the wooden slats of the bridge and looked up at him. She opened her eyes as wide as she could to contain her tears but was still left with the sensation of peering through windows dripping with condensation.

'Are you all right?' she said.

Max noted the tremor in her voice, the restless bottom lip, the swollen eyes; and assured her he was perfectly fine. 'Now, there's two little blighters who could do with a little less adventure and a bit more poetry!'

But she was not bluffed by his words or the smile that accompanied them. She returned his smile, she hoped with more conviction, and hid beneath her parasol.

They continued silently in the direction of Oxford's sun-spotted spires and turrets, she pondering how so meek a man was now duty-bound to inflict pain and death for his country and he torturing himself with the suspicion she was too perceptive not to have detected his soft streak in the course of the *contretemps*.

'Such wanton cruelty and suffering disturbs you greatly, doesn't it? Even in a dumb animal like that poor rabbit,' she said eventually, as they drew abreast of the college barges and boathouses abutting Christ Church Meadow. 'I could see the sadness in your eyes, see it afflicting your whole body.'

Max felt that familiar heaving in his stomach. She had only spent a few hours in his company and had seen through him already, right through to a core as brittle as a maggoty crab apple. He ran a finger under his collar, his mind racing ahead, imagining the scene back in the mess when Peter Revell relates the story of Lanham and the bunny-rabbit to a sniggering audience. Christ Almighty!

'Well, I know this will sound awfully wet, but I used to keep pet rabbits as a boy, you see . . .'

'You don't have to answer.'

Max looked across at her, twirling her parasol, striding out coltishly, eyes fixed on some distant speck, secure in her own stillness. He wanted to hold her close and tight in the hope he might absorb some of that peace.

'I find it invigorating in a man,' she said flatly. 'These days there's too much emphasis laid on playing the man, stiff upper lip and all that—whatever that's supposed to mean. Look where that gets us?'

She did not wait for an answer. And max was not moved to offer one. He could see she had only posed the rhetorical question to take his mind off the rabbit.

'I wonder what cakes they have at the Clarendon today?' she continued to similar purpose. 'I'm really quite famished after all this walking! Aren't you?'

Max patted his stomach. He knew what she had done and thanked her for it under his breath.

'You may have to start praying,' he said. 'What with the flour shortage and the price of bread going up, you'll be lucky to find bread and jam!'

They dawdled over Folly Bridge and up St Aldates, halting to admire Christ Church's Tom Tower and discuss how Henry VIII had mistreated Wolsey, before crossing Carfax and walking down Cornmarket to the Clarendon.

Max ordered the set tea, which amounted to two thin slices of buttered bread and a dollop of plum jam that lost nothing in comparison to the tasteless tinned variety they got at the front. The cake she had so craved turned out to be small Nelson square; Max derived so much pleasure from watching her bite through the thin pastry crust into the dark and spicy fruit sponge beneath with the gusto of an appreciative toddler that he passed her his slice. This disappointingly meagre fare failed to dampen their lively conversation, however, which went on to encompass subjects as diverse as her passion for opera and his regard for DH Lawrence's new novel *Sons and Lovers*.

When the long-case clock in the corner chimed six, Max called for the bill and insisted they return to Iffley by taxi-cab since she must be exhausted. At first she desisted because she did not want their expedition to end any sooner than it must. Eventually they shook hands at the gate of Nowell House and parted, each of them too self-conscious to air the possibility of a further meeting, both wary of rejection spoiling an almost perfect day.

Rowan Hawes went inside without a backward glance and informed Mrs Beenham of her lovely day spent in the delightful company of a young officer. Then she went straight upstairs to her room and threw herself full length onto the bed. She took her journal from the bedside pedestal, giggled and, in a sweeping hand, confided that Peter Revell may have inadvertently presented a rival for her affections.

Max, meanwhile, was walking back to Lawn Upton in a state foreign to him, one he was given no option but to identify as euphoria. The air seemed cleaner; the leaves on the trees greener; the tune of an evening songbird so uplifting that he began whistling *If you were the only girl in the world* in reply.

A few hours in the company of a girl he had just met for the first time could not be responsible? Or could it? Yes, she was pretty. But not in any extravagant way; she was not a head-turner like Zena Boas. She was definitely intelligent and well read. But, thankfully, not to the brink of boorishness like Vanessa Devereux. She seemed to listen and care. Either that or she had mastered the art of appearing so. Damn it! His mind was whirling faster than a carousel at St Giles' Fair!

And there was one other thing. Not once had the war ever been mentioned. Not one concession in six hours to bombardments, night patrols, incompetent superiors and truculent men, lousy food or lousy bodies. There was another world out there. A world of untarnished beauty, full of simple pleasures and joyous companionship. Another world he might inhabit and enjoy—if only he could survive this damned war. This girl had banished his pain quicker than a shot of morphine.

Max could not get her out of his head. And, if that's the case, he asked himself, what was he going to do about it?

10

Holywell Street

Max was reading the *Collected Works of Lord Byron* when Rufey entered the library with a letter: 'Delivered by hand, Master Max. The boy's waiting, should there be a reply.'

It was from Rowan Hawes: there was a concert at the Holywell Music Room that evening, a recital of Italian operatic arias by Verdi and Puccini to be performed by the tenor Carlo Umberto and the soprano Livia Edita; 'Mrs Beenham is unwell and Mr Beenham is reluctant to leave her . . . I know it's short notice and opera may not be to your taste, but would you care to escort me?'

Opera was not really to Max's 'taste' but nothing was going to prevent him from ringing the doorbell of Nowell House at seven o'clock as requested.

Unless, he surmised, it was the lack of appropriate apparel for an operatic recital. He sprang from his chair and, negotiating the stairs two at a time, went directly to his wardrobe and began rummaging at the back where he suspected his evening suit was hiding. His nose puckered with the pungency of liberated mothballs as he hung the suit on the back of the door for inspection: evidence of a half-decent chianti on the lapel confirmed his hunch that it had not been cleaned since his 21ˢᵗ birthday supper, but he put his faith in a thorough sponge down and a gentle brushing followed by a long airing on the clothes line outside being sufficient to make it presentable. If not, he would be forced to fall back on his uniform once again—and that was looking even more tired.

'Mother!' he shouted. 'I need the car tonight! All right?'

His mother came to the foot of the staircase. 'The car? Why, no, I'm afraid not. I'm motoring over to Garsington to dine with the Crooks . . .'

'Ah, yes, Crooks by name . . .'

'That will do, Max!' said his mother, an octave higher.

She had hoped the opportunity to chastise her son would arise at a moment of her choosing but his behaviour since coming home had already provoked one of her persistent headaches.

'Max, you really are the limit,' she said icily. 'You throw what I can only describe as a neurotic fit in front of our guests and disappear in the most discourteous manner. It needed all my diplomacy to avoid an extremely embarrassing situation.'

'Speak for yourself, mother. I wasn't embarrassed one iota!'

'It may interest you to know that while you were gallivanting off somewhere all day yesterday your mother was confined to bed with such headaches that Doctor Clubb had to be called.'

'Of no interest at all, if you must know,' Max replied routinely. 'But we don't want to cripple you with another beastly headache, do we? I'll telephone for a taxi-cab.'

'Max!'

She heard her son's departing footsteps on the landing and a faint 'Enjoy your dinner' before his bedroom door slammed shut. Max spent the rest of the day avoiding her by taking the Byron anthology into the glade and counting the minutes to his departure. On his way out, however, an idea prompted a brief detour into the library.

He waited until the seventh chime of Iffley's church-bell had died away before activating Nowell House's shriller version. He was re-acquainted with the sitting room by the maid and, while waiting for Rowan Hawes to appear, stood legs akimbo in front of the fireplace, hands twiddling behind his back, too anxious to sit down. He leant forward to appraise himself in the mirror, and wondered what she would make of his effort to spruce himself up; and, more importantly, to ponder what she would be wearing and how she would look. Had his beauty-deprived brain been playing tricks with him on that river walk?

He heard a swish of satin and turned to behold a vision that momentarily ambushed thought and speech. She looked spectacular in a two-tone green frock that dropped to the floor from beneath her bosom, its sheen complementing the sparkle in her eyes and setting off the fire in her auburn hair which was coiffed into a chignon and secured with what appeared to be a pin encrusted with emeralds—though he assumed they could only be paste. The pin complemented the heart broach pinned to her left breast below the strap.

'My, you look ravishing!' Max said, scarcely unable to believe his eyes or his luck. At that moment Cupid did not have enough arrows in his quiver to fulfill his needs.

She let out a theatrical sigh, for she had spent an hour at her dressing table toying with her make-up and had tried on three different outfits before finally deciding on this one.

'A concert like this doesn't occur often these days so I wanted to make the most of it.'

Max held up his hands in mock surrender. 'As indeed you have!'

He wanted desperately to look at her when he said it but he could feel himself, quite literally, getting hot under the collar. He tugged at his white tie.

'Here, let me see?' she said as natural as could be, pinching either end between her fingers and giving a short, sharp pull. 'There, that's better!'

'Thank you.'

'How do I look?' she said, retreating to a safer distance. 'Will I do?'

Her cheekbones bore only the slightest traces of rouge, her skin carried only the lightest dusting of powder, and her lips shone pink. But it was those green eyes, as bright as a beacon in a storm, that drew Max in. She had taken the trouble to separate her eyelashes with a pin after applying mascara, but not on the lower lashes for she believed it cast a shadow and gave the impression of bags beneath her eyes. And her perfume seemed to inhabit every pore and every strand of hair so that she smelt like Max thought an angel must smell: the trick, acquired from her mother, of adding a few drops of scent to her hair after rinsing had worked to perfection.

Had Max been a cat he would have licked her. As it was, he just stared over her shoulder worrying where to put his arms should she stand her ground much longer.

'I feel a complete scruff compared to you!' he said, rubbing sweaty palms on the seat of his trousers. 'I can only apologize for the state of this suit of mine.'

She looked at his suit and nodded behind a smile.

'But my old headmaster always told us that it's hair, finger-nails and shoes that denote a gentleman,' said Max, extending his hands and lifting a boot.

'You'll pass!' she said and meant it: he looked as dashing as she had fantasized. 'Shall we go?'

Max put his hand in his pocket. 'I've no *corsage* for you but I do have a small memento of the evening.'

He extricated a slim book and held it out for her to take. He hoped she might accept it with a kiss.

'Thank you so much!' she said, quite taken by surprise. 'My God, it's beautiful. Look at this scarlet leather! So smooth! It's hardly worn!'

She opened the book at the title page and her hand went to her mouth as Max wagered it might. 'Byron's *Hebrew Melodies*! Dated 1815! Where on earth did you get a wonderful edition like this? It must have cost a fortune!'

Max's cheeks began to mirror the leather. 'Well, to tell the truth, it came from our library. I thought we'd some Yeats, but sadly I was mistaken. So I found you this instead.'

'I can't possibly keep it. What would your parents say?'

'They'll not even notice it's missing,' said Max abruptly. 'I insist you keep it, and perhaps when you read it you'll spare a thought for me out in the trenches.'

At this moment she yearned to go further: she wanted to embrace him. Peter Revell never gave her books: he'd only once given her a surprise gift, held her hand in public or declared his love for her. To own such a book as this filled her with such joy that she longed to leap into Max's arms and kiss him full on the lips but all she contrived was to mouth another hushed 'Thank you.'

Max reacted to the lack of tangible reward with a thin smile that reflected both his disappointment and years of rigorously enforced social graces. He, like Peter Revell, was hamstrung by diffidence, terrified by the fear of rejection, unsure how to read the female condition or decipher its signals. The outcome was a bashfulness so acute it could easily be mistaken for rudeness.

The possibility of further embarrassment was forestalled by the taxi-cab arriving as scheduled. The evening was warm so she had elected to wear just a shawl which Max draped around her shoulders, catching a whiff of her perfume and a tantalizing glimpse of skin that made his lascivious *alter ego* want to nip her neck. He visualized his lips wandering from her neck to her ear lobes and finally to her mouth but in reality they became chained to a babbling sequence of inane observations about the buildings lining the Iffley Road. It seemed the harder he sought to rekindle the rapport of their riverside walk the more tortuous his manner became. He began to think that his only course was to abandon all caution and launch himself at her.

Fortunately, Max lacked the necessary bravado for that; and the time. Inside ten minutes they had crossed The Plain and Magdalen Bridge and turned right toward Holywell Street where the Music Room, an unostentatious stone edifice, both without and within, lay on the right hand side just beyond the gates of New College.

'The Room was opened in 1748 with a performance of Handel's *Oratorio of Eshter*,' she said breathlessly as the taxi drew up outside. 'It's the earliest building to be dedicated solely to music in the whole of Europe!'

She handed Max the tickets and he, in turn, passed them to the usher who indicated their seats. Max bought two programmes and they settled down to read them until the commencement of the recital enabled them to pursue their individual agendas: her eyes and ears were focused on the performances while his senses treated them as background music because they were focused entirely upon her. He never took his eyes off her, unless he thought she was about to say something to him whereupon he would quickly stare down at his programme and appear completely lost in the music.

He smiled with her throughout Umberto's rendition of *La donna e mobile* but was instantly nonplussed when Edita's very first note of *Vissi d'arte* reduced her to tears. He consulted the programme: 'A cruel police chief demands Tosca yield to his advances if she wishes for the release of her imprisoned lover . . . in her dilemma she prays to heaven, asking why she should be treated so harshly when her whole life has been dedicated to music, love and doing good works.'

Then, quite inexplicably, everything around him seemed to still. The bows of the string players motionless; the soprano's mouth frozen.

For what seemed an eternity, but amounted to barely thirty seconds, the universe, his world, was stuck in suspended animation. The only disturbance were the thoughts thrumming inside his brain. And everything, everything that mattered, suddenly became clearer to him.

What if opera was a metaphor for life? His life? Here was his life being bared to the bone: its injustices resonating in the aching vocal instrument of the soprano's voice; its repressed emotion crying out in every one of Rowan Hawes's tears. Here was a loudspeaker to the soul; passion writ large. If he could learn anything from opera about how to live his life, Max deduced, it was to give a voice to the emotions he kept imprisoned within his soul. Some of those liberated might be greeted as demons. But he could not help that. It was time to be true only unto himself. He could not understand why this suddenly made sense, but he realized it was as much a fact as two and two making four. And from such basic principles did greater things evolve.

Max gazed at Rowan Hawes with renewed insight and recognized another spirit struggling for freedom: her hands wringing in her lap; her chest rising and falling to every note. He squeezed her wrist and gave her feelings release; took charge of them and gave her passion a home. Her eyes followed its flight, and, as the soprano's last tremulous note died away, she bent over and kissed him on the cheek.

Max experienced every square inch of skin come alive with an exquisite attack of pins and needles. All peripheral vision had shut down; all he saw was her face. This vision of beauty and mystery drew him in as perilously as any quicksand. This must be what love felt like. What being loved felt like. He felt he was seconds away from making an ass of himself. But it no longer mattered.

'Oh, Max, I may call you Max?' she sighed, as they got into the waiting taxi. 'Thank you for a lovely evening.'

His mouth opened to pour out words of love, but all he heard himself say was a pathetically lame 'the pleasure was mine.'

Max's eyes never left her as she reached into her bag and freshened her face with a sheet of *papier poudre*. Her skin seemed to be lit from within, every freckle burnished gold. His stare caused her to drop the bag. She read his mind. She watched his pupils dilate and realized her slightest initiative would be reciprocated. And once she heard the words of Byron she knew she would provide one.

'She walks in beauty, like the night . . .' he recited, at last finding words to do justice to what he was feeling.

'Of cloudless climes and starry nights,' she responded huskily.

She responded to the beat of her heart by laying her head tenderly against his shoulder until it rested where the neck met the hairline behind the ear and his mouth. Feeling no resistance, he kissed the lobe. She slid her arms around his neck and the first kiss was like two butterflies colliding. But the second was different. It wasn't a courtesy kiss for an escort; nor a friend's kiss. It was a lover's kiss, open-mouthed, probing, hungry for more.

They remained entwined in each other's embrace all the way to Iffley, inwardly relieved that the unspoken had been broached and glad at the outcome. Yet few endearments passed between them, for if love had ensnared them, it had done so unwittingly. It constituted a forbidden love, a tiny wet flame they could neither hold nor throw away. Their love amounted to an act of treachery. They shared one last, languorous kiss; their lips rejecting numerous chances to part, sensing there might never be another.

With the cab driver demanding his fare, part they must and, in so doing, her emerald broach caught in his lapel.

'Why do you always wear this broach?' he asked, walking her to the door. 'Is it a particular favourite? An heirloom?'

She hesitated before answering, wondering whether to tell the truth or not.

'Peter gave it to me the night before he left for France,' she said eventually.

Max smiled weakly. Reality had come back to bite the head off his dreams.

'You remember what they said about Byron, don't you?' he said.

'What's that?'

'Mad, bad and dangerous to know!'

'Of course!' she laughed.

'Well, so am I.'

A smile illuminated Rowan's face like a Halloween lantern: here was a man who could make her laugh and cry in the same sentence. But was this dangerous yearning, this *amour fou* she felt raging inside her, genuine or just the bliss of a cloudburst after a prolonged drought?

She dared herself to challenge her feelings by inviting him inside. But she was afraid where they might lead.

She hurried inside and once safely within the citadel of her bedroom, she pressed her back against the door, removed Revell's love token and finally surrendered to the tears that were eating away at her conscience like acid rain: unforgiving, burning, relentless.

Max watched her disappear into the house. The stars twinkling above its chimneys seemed to him like holes in the floor of heaven through which he could glimpse paradise. He thought of pursuing her, hammering on the door and professing his love for her: a wild and passionate love startling in its rawness. But his legs seemed already mired in that Flanders mud which lay in wait for him. He plodded homeward, kicking out at stones and slashing hedgerows with a hawthorn switch, despair and desolation snapping at his heels like two black dogs, as forlorn as the Last Post played on a cracked bugle.

Max reached Lawn Upton and crept up to his room. He slipped his jacket on its hanger and smelt her perfume lingering in its fabric. He caressed the garment as if he were soaping her naked shoulders and watched as his fingertips collected the strands of hair she had left there. Fetching an envelope from his desk, he wound them into a lover's knot and placed them inside.

He knew he had no grounds for hoping his love might be reciprocated. She was spoken for; she had plans and aspirations. He, by contrast, had no direction in his life and few qualities likely to provide any should he survive this war apart from a modest talent to amuse and a certain way with words—minor attributes for a future in civilian life and ones he was apt to overplay shamelessly. How could he possibly expect to mine a gem beyond rubies.

Whatever their destiny held, he knew one place where he might find her.

'Goodnight Rowan,' he whispered as his eyes closed and he waited for sleep. 'Stay strong. Sleep tight.'

She smiled back at him: her smile, unlike any other, slightly askew, born behind the eyes, a smile that dazzled like the morning sun bouncing off snowy mountain tops, its warmth capable of melting away the coldest anguish.

He waited for her to speak, but she said nothing and, turning her head away, slipped silently from view.

11

The Shallows

The metallic noise rattled inside Max's skull like the whirr of a Verey shell and tumbled him out of bed. His eyes opened on a ceiling bathed in yellow light. But it was sunlight not flame. His breathing eased. He got to his feet and went over to the window; there in the drive below was Bert Clack's milk wagon. Beside it was the gawky figure of Chick Collicutt in the act of retrieving the churn he had just dropped off the tailgate.

'Morning, Chick!' he called, leaning out of the window.

'Master Max! Heard you was 'ome!' Chick shouted back, stepping on the lid of the churn and being loudly rebuked by Clack, who was left shaking a trouser leg doused with milk.

Chick ran over to the path below Max's bedroom window. 'The perch are bitin' below San'ford lasher. I'm goin' down later. Comin?'

'Then I don't see why a proper fisherman shouldn't catch the blighters!' joked Max. 'I'll drop by the pub in, what, an hour?'

'You bet!' Chick replied, touching his cap.

Max sucked in the dizzy smells of summer drifting up from the garden along with on rising sun. The smell of working horse and leather harness joined them as Chick and the cart disappeared down the drive. Max chuckled at the sight of Chick, half-walking, half-skipping, like a knock-kneed foal. Chick must be 16 now, he calculated, yet he still looked more boy than youth. In his shabby black cord jacket and trousers, his arms and legs looked like long sticks of liquorish, having completely outgrown his torso. Since the size of Chick's feet and head—apart from the fleshy strawberry nose that had taken control of his facial features—had also failed to keep pace with his limbs, his appearance left him vulnerable to mild joshing if he was fortunate or vicious taunting if he were not: and acting more boy than youth only tended to invite the latter.

The opportunity to ditch his uniform in favour of something less formal and infinitely more comfortable came as some relief to Max in a month that was beginning to live up to its epithet of 'Flaming June', and he quickly slipped into the faded blue canvas trousers and blue gingham cotton shirt he always wore for a spot of summer fishing before contemplating breakfast.

In the dining room below, Max's parents had heard the commotion outside, which likewise drew his mother to the window. 'It's that creature from the public house,' she sniffed.

The germ of a tiny smile began to form on her husband's lugubrious features. He rose from his chair to have a look for himself, but neither he nor the smile was allowed to get any further.

'Sit down, Roy,' commanded his wife. 'I imagine Mrs Tedder will finally send some coffee now the milk has arrived.'

A further delay did nothing to ease Naomi Lanham's displeasure, and she filled her time by moving on to one of her favourite subjects, believing wholeheartedly in the adage 'there's a time and place for everything'—so long as it was she who chose the time and the place.

'Why does Max have to consort with that . . . boy,' she said, laying enough stress on the last word to strangle it. 'It's unhealthy, a grown man hanging around with a 16-year-old like that. People talk.'

Her husband spooned kedgeree onto a plate with the zest of a fireman shovelling coal on the footplate of The Flying Scotsman. 'Yes, my dear.'

'If it were in my power I'd have the mother thrown out of that public house tomorrow. I've told Tinegate to have a word with the licensing committee.'

Roy Lanham attempted a scowl. 'Is that really necessary?'

'Do close your mouth! You look like a pony in mid-chew!'

Her husband sat down and began eating his breakfast impervious to his wife's continuing harangue.

'Max really does infuriate. Do you know, Tinegate passed him in St Aldates the other day and Max completely ignored him. Looked straight through him. He was with a woman, needless to add.'

'Really . . .'

'Rather better class than Zena Boas from what I can make out.'

She looked to her husband but he gave nothing away.

'I know he visits that Boas girl.'

She paused and glared at him. 'If a gentleman must sew his wild oats he ought at least to have the good sense and common courtesy to sew them in a field far from his own!'

Naomi Lanham buttered her toast with mounting ferocity. 'So, who is this other woman? Max has not mentioned anyone to me. Do you happen to know her?'

'No.'

'Doesn't he realize how rude his behaviour looks? Sometimes I think this came at an opportune moment for him, gave him some purpose, because he seems to have no appreciation of how to get on in life. He can be so dismissive.'

'Just shyness, I think. Easily confused with aloofness or even rudeness by those who fail to understand.'

'Why must people try to understand him!' she exclaimed. 'He's not a child any longer. He ought to know better. We brought him up properly, didn't we?'

Her husband put down his knife and fork and searched for the courage to speak out, but all his tongue found was a grain of rice stuck between his teeth.

'God forbid he should come to any harm in this war,' she continued, 'but what on earth is he going to do with himself once it's over if this is the way he treats people of good standing in the community? It's high time he found a nice girl!'

'Vanessa Devereux, by any chance?'

She looked across as if she'd spotted a caterpillar crawling in his kedgeree.

'It's high time he found . . . a nice girl! And gave me a grandchild. If he's not dreadfully careful he'll end up leading the same dissolute existence you did before I came to your rescue.'

Her irritation was quelled by her son's entry, then instantly re-ignited by sight of his apparel. 'I suppose this means you're going fishing with that Collicutt boy?'

'I am indeed!' Max replied cheerfully, and flashed a wide smile which he knew would make her feel even more infuriated. 'Why don't you come father? The perch are biting!'

Roy Lanham lay a forkful of kedgeree back down on his plate. He felt his heart pounding like a tom-tom against his waistcoat.

'Your father hasn't the time for such frivolities.'

'Don't be so silly, mother,' snapped Max.

'How dare you talk to me like that in front of your father!' she snapped back.

Max squared his shoulders. 'I'll talk to you how I like. I'm not some boy you can browbeat any longer!'

His mother visibly trembled. 'And keep your voice down . . .'

'Or the servants will hear?' Max said in a snide voice. 'It'll get round the village that the Lanhams don't get on with each other? That we aren't the perfect little family we're supposed to be? Oh, come on, mother! They know everything there is worth knowing about us, right down to your dress size!'

Max grinned reassurance toward his father, but Roy Lanham's head hung as limply as a weakly hinged gate, his eyes fixed on his plate, glistening with a pain he was vainly struggling to conceal.

'You've plenty of time on your hands, haven't you father?'

Max stared at his father, imploring him to say 'Yes'; desperately trying to plant the word in his head. Just this once, he pleaded. You know you want to, father. I've made an effort. Now it's your turn.

His father lit a cigarette, and was convulsed by a hacking cough. Max had never seen the attraction of smoking, and the sight of his father's rocking head and the smell of his rancid breath was enough to remind him of the reasons why.

'Let's get some air, father.'

Max led him out onto the lawn. He studied his father, who looked every inch the executive in a smart grey suit and striped tie even though he had not sat at his desk in the family's Cowley engineering factory for 15 years or more. Perhaps not exactly every inch: Max noticed how his trouser legs flapped like spent balloons and the collar of his crisp blue shirt that had once been so snug now seemed a size too big.

'You need to gain some weight.'

'You don't need much weight to knock in small nails!'

'What?'

'I have all the energy I need,' his father answered, picking tobacco off his tongue.

'There's a lot of life out there for you if only you'd go out and grab it!'

'Your mother says . . .'

'My mother talks tommyrot!' fumed Max. 'And you know it!'

'Fine for you to say. You don't have to live with her all the time.'

'But this is your house, your home! You're the master here!'

His father coughed, exhaling clouds of smoke. 'Try telling your mother that.'

Roy Lanham had tried telling her, had tried to play the master. But it never lasted long. He was wealthy and he knew she would never leave him, but it added no steel his backbone. He was content to let things lie. This was one of the very few things he absolutely knew and understood. He knew about fishing and about horse-racing; he knew a bit about motor cars. Most of all he knew his wife was still a considerable beauty who might take her pick of numerous rakes. But he also knew he had too much money for her ever to leave him. In any circumstances. Of that he was certain because it had been tested.

Max circled him angrily. 'When was the last time you attended a match? Cricket, rugby or football?'

'God, I can't recall. Ages ago, I expect.'

'And why? After all those years you played them.'

'Yes, best days of my life. Young, carefree, pockets full of money, girl on each arm!'

'I know those days can never return. But you mustn't just sit back and fade away.'

'Wait for the grim reaper, eh?'

'That's one way of putting it, yes.'

'I've made my bed, Max, and I must sleep on it.'

Max's mouth twisted into the contemptuous smile a son reserves for a father. 'You're the second man to say that to me this week. It's defeatist talk.'

'I'm dreadfully sorry . . .'

'If that's to be your outlook on life, then it's me who should be feeling sorry for you!' Max interjected loudly. 'To hell with you! I'm late. I must go.'

Max stormed back to the house, via the kitchen, to collect his fishing gear, throwing floats, reels, leads and lines into his bag with no thought for their fragility. He grabbed his rod and made a slamming exit out of the front door for maximum effect. He realized he was behaving like a tot denied the last toffee in the bag but he did not care. A square peg in a round hole at the front and a round peg in a square hole at home. Did he fit in anywhere in this world? Was there nowhere he might find peace?

Chick was waiting for him outside The George and greeted him with a wave.

'There, told you. Knew he wuz gonner come!' he shouted to his mother, who was standing in the doorway.

'Good morning, Mrs Collicutt,' said Max, touching his forelock. 'Nice day!'

Years running a pub had destroyed any natural beauty Chick's mother possessed, weariness seeming to hang heavily from her every feature. She had managed to retain her firm jaw line and her smooth skin but the latter's one-time peachiness was now reduced to the colour of onion paper, stretched so thin as to be translucent. Her hair was a tightserpent's nest of greying curls showing few traces of the golden hue his father had described her having when she took over the pub just after Chick was born. By that time Mr Collicutt had disappeared, leaving her to bring up the boy alone.

She pursed her lips, already wrinkled from decades of cigarette smoking, until they reminded Max of walnut shells. 'You keep an eye on him, Master Max. I don't waunt no harm comin' to 'im.'

Max dragged away her red-faced son with a smile, and the pair set off down the Sandford road, past the smithy.

Albert Bostock had heard their conversation and was lurking outside, wearing a face as black as an Angus bull's.

'You've bin threatnin' my boy Eddie,' he growled.

'Is that a question or a statement of fact, Mister Bostock?' Max replied curtly.

'Down the river, other art'noon. You an' some oity-toity woman.'

Max got close enough to the blacksmith to negate any swing he might entertain.

'Mister Bostock,' he said in as low a register as he could muster, 'your Eddie is developing into the same kind of nasty, petty thug as his elder brother and will be treated as he deserves. If you've a complaint, take it to Constable Treadaway.'

Max made to walk away.

'An' stay away from Zena Boas!'

'I beg your pardon!' Max hissed, turning back.

'She's spoke for . . .'

'Spoken for! Are you losing your mind? By how many?'

'When our Hector gets to 'ear of it,' Bostock sneered, 'I don't waunner be in your boots! He lands a tasty punch . . . you'd be greedy to ask for more!'

He sniggered at his joke and went back inside the forge, but the heavy clunk of metal on metal hammered its message around Max's brain until long after he and Chick had crossed over the railway bridge and passed the asylum gates. As they walked on down the hill toward Sandford, Chick admitted to having had 'one or two run-ins' with Eddie Bostock and in spite of his lurid descriptions Max deduced from his head-down, hands-in-pockets slouch that he had not come off best.

They turned right at The Fox and headed past St Andrews church toward the river, pinpointed by the chimney of the paper mill beside the lock, as towering a Sandford landmark as the Laundry's chimney was to Littlemore. Max dug tuppence out of his trouser pocket for the toll bridge by the King's Arms: why it should be twice as much as Iffley's tax, he'd never managed to fathom.

The roar of the lasher could be heard in all its foaming, violent glory. They walked toward the noise and crossed the main lasher stream at Fiddlers Elbow to reach The Shallows, a small stream eventually traversed by a wooden footbridge where it met the main river channel at a smaller weir. Chick quickened his step and pointed to the wooden piers. 'Thass where they are! Round the bottom o' the stakes!'

The chose their spot after shooing away a herd of foraging Ayrshires: they'd wandered over from the far meadows, toward Kennington, that were already parched by the summer sun to feed off the last tufts of lush grass from the spring floods. Chick began spraying ground bait into the water with the sweeping arm of a seasoned practitioner while Max set up the rods and laid out the floats and bait.

Chick declared he wanted to make a contest of the day: a chocolate bar to the winner; only perch to count. Max humoured him, and agreed. Chick was soon filling his keep net with perch after perch, greeting each prickly-finned and orange-striped catch with a teenage whoop as he adjusted the score even more in his favour. Max caught the odd perch and a few gudgeon. He didn't sit back and allow Chick to win their contest, but he was happy to see him happy.

The hot hours passed to a Thames symphony: the sound of plopping moorhens, hooting swans and buzzing wasps performed against a backcloth of floating dandelion seeds and the smell of baking dung. Throughout this rustic idyll Max was preoccupied with more important matters than deciding whether to bait his hook with paste or worm or where best to cast his line or how the succession of wispy clouds scudding across the sky resembled famous faces. His thoughts were full of Rowan Hawes; but they were as jumbled as the worms in his bait tin. And yet there was really only one issue to unravel: how he might get to see her again before he left tomorrow.

After Chick had defeated the ants in the battle to devour the last of the cheese and piccalilli sandwiches—Max professed lack of appetite as he loathed both cheese and the ghastly yellow chutney—that Mrs Collicutt had provided for them, they returned their catch to the river and packed up their gear. 'Looks black over Iffley,' said Chick. 'Storm comin', I reck'n.' Even so, Max suggested they go upriver and walk home via Iffley.

The towpath took them under the brooding mass that was the Black Bridge, now even more glowering thanks to the approaching storm clouds. One defiant shaft of sunlight was streaming through the westernmost of the three giant arches like a lighthouse beam. Max blinked, and thought he saw a lone figure on the parapet being goaded by others from below. And he felt again the terrors of a distant summer night.

'Have you jumped yet?' he asked.

Chick screwed-up his face. 'Thought 'bout it . . . bin up . . .'

Max finished the sentence for him. 'But not yet.'

They paused beneath the girders, coated with soot and streaked with rivulets of rust, and not for the first time Max wondered how this heap of old iron—marvellous piece of engineering though it was—could assume such mythical proportions in the local psyche.

'Doesn't look so big from down here, does it?' said Max. 'Bit different when you're up top though?'

'You en't arf kiddin',' Chick replied, with a nervous chuckle. 'Thought I wuz goin' to pee me pants when I looked over the edge!'

They both laughed out loud, the noise echoing around the girders like a cough in a church.

Chick frowned, debating whether to pose his next question. 'What's it really loik?' he said after a pause heavy with nervousness. 'Jumpin', I mean.'

Max smiled. He frequently convinced himself he was not quite the smart arse he was accused of being, but on this occasion the charge was accurate: he knew the subject was always going to be raised. He could think of no reason why Chick should not hear the truth.

'The test of the Black Bridge is just an artificial rite of passage . . .'

'A what?'

'A test to prove you're a man not a child. It has no real substance.'

'Oh,' said Chick, disappointed.

'It proves nothing. It's childish to believe otherwise. It's a stupid thing to do in the first place and no one should ever feel obliged to behave in a certain way, to do something because it's the done thing.'

Chick ruffled his wayward hair into a greater tangle. Max's rationale had meant nothing to him. The consequences of it did. 'But what about ar'terwards, if you don't jump?'

Max raised his eyebrows. 'The ribbing? The merciless taunts in the street? The cruel comments chalked on gates?'

Chick lowered his chin. 'S'pose, yes.'

'Simple, Chick,' Max said loudly and solemnly. 'You ignore them. They serve no purpose to those that hurl them if you show that they've not hit home.'

'Dunno whether I could do that,' mumbled Chick. 'If I'd failed a test o' courage, prob'ly 'ave to agree I wuz a coward.'

'Believe me, Chick,' Max emphasized with a shake of his head, 'sometimes it takes greater courage to stand out against the crowd, to say "No" rather than follow the herd. The greatest courage of all is the courage of the individual against the mob.'

'Stand up for what you thinks, you mean?'

'Yes, that's about the size of it,' Max conceded with a sigh. 'Don't give-in to your peers, your mates, if you don't want to, if you disagree with them. Don't be browbeaten, don't give-in to bullying—physical or mental. If a cause is not worth fighting for, keep your hands in your pockets. That's real courage, moral courage, the courage of your convictions. The courage to answer only to your conscience.'

Chick stood up straighter and taller. 'Thass easier to say when you're a war 'ero an' all . . .'

Max's expression went from grave to grim, causing Chick to inspect the ground at his feet: he didn't like to see Master Max sad; more so if he'd been the cause. He felt Max place a hand on his chest. 'Every man out there is a hero, Chick. Arthur Goodey, Sam Dewe. Even Hector bloody Bostock!'

Chick's mouth tightened. 'Can't wait to go!' he blurted, eyes shining.

'Don't wish for something you may find you did not want!' Max said angrily, pushing Chick backwards 'Don't ask me to tell you more or explain. But you just pray this thing ends before you're nineteenth birthday!'

Chick's lower lip trembled. His only wish was to earn Max's praise. He shuffled his feet and nibbled his bottom lip. Sadness soaked through him as if he were a lump of limestone. He could not understand why Max had got so cross. Wearing the khaki, shooting and bayoneting the Boche with your pals must be fun, mustn't it? And if he didn't go soon it would be all over. The Black Bridge would always be there, but this war would end.

Max didn't want Chick's obvious disappointment to ruin his day. 'Let's get you your prize, shall we? Keep your fingers crossed that machine at Iffley hasn't run out of chocolate bars! And hope those clouds don't burst on us! On the way I'll tell you what really happened the day I jumped the Black Bridge . . .'

Chick was not listening. 'Woss that?' he said. 'Over there, in the copse.'

Max tracked the line of Chick's gaze and spotted a patch of coloured cloth lying on the ground, a shirt or a dress. Suddenly, it moved. The two of them cautiously moved from tree to tree until they were close enough to identify what it was.

It was a shirt. And a dress. A couple were lying in the undergrowth, the gentle swish of the late afternoon breeze in the tree tops a whispering counterpoint to their energetic coupling.

Chick stood as slack-jawed and wide-eyed as a startled chimpanzee; and moved away only reluctantly when Max ordered him to. But Max's own body refused to move, his eyes riveted upon the man's milky buttocks thrusting back and forth in tune with the flailing movements of his woman's spread-eagled legs, his grunts harmonizing with her gasps. Max's mouth went dry, but the rest of him began to sweat so freely he could feel the cotton shirt sticking to the small of his back where trickles of perspiration had begun to collect. He watched them finish and then slunk away, head down, unable even to derive a voyeur's pleasure, feeling closer to a sick nosey parker who has stumbled across someone's diary and drooled over their lecherous confessions.

Max rejoined Chick, sulking on the towpath, and began marching as if he were leading his platoon toward a rest area behind the lines. They reached Iffley in double-quick time, but despite taking the long route around the village he told Chick it was too late to make the detour to the chocolate machine and that he would give him his winnings tomorrow. Of Rowan Hawes there was no sign. How stupid could he be? Why would she be wandering the streets at this hour?

They stopped outside Nowell House. The air was still and there was hardly a sound aside from Max's laboured breathing. Then he thought he detected her voice from within. He put his hand on the gate but could not, would not, go any farther. He slammed a fist into his thigh and turned away, dragging a bemused Chick with him. Each step Max took away from her only made him hotter and more wound-up.

Max and Chick parted at The George as dusk was falling. Instead of heading to Lawn Upton, Max cast a swift glance over each shoulder and ran across the road.

He found Zena in the kitchen, preparing supper. Grabbing her by the hand, he quashed her surprise with a kiss and dragged her upstairs, stopping on the landing to force her against the wall and kiss her again, this time behind the ear. They fell backwards through the bedroom door onto the bed, and he began tugging at her clothes, ripping away the buttons that would not give.

Zena had never known him consumed by such naked passion but her astonishment rapidly turned into a nail-digging ferocity of her own.

He was like a stranger on top of her: urgent, demanding, animal-like in his frenzy. She felt Max was hers, finally and completely hers.

She was mistaken. For although the body writhing beneath his belonged to her, the face Max was anointing with a lover's kisses belonged to Rowan Hawes.

12

Noeux

Three years of war had raised the Army's routine organization to such a peak of efficiency that after breakfasting at Lawn Upton Max was back with his battalion just outside Arras by nightfall.

He had passed the journey gazing out of the carriage window, lost in his own thoughts, thinking of what lay behind him rather than ahead. Rowan Hawes looked out from every passing cloud: he smelt her perfume on every breeze; instead of anunforgiving head-rest he felt the soft white pillow of her neck and shoulders. Yet it left him feeling afraid. A different kind of fear than the usual. No longer the soldier's fear of a slow and painful death. It was life he was afraid of now. By giving him a reason to stay alive Rowan Hawes ensured every day would be harder than the last.

Max rejoined the Battalion at Noeux where it was enjoying a midsummer respite in billets and undergoing training as part of GHQ reserve. The village was a new one to Max, but something about it stirred his imagination. It was a pretty collection of houses gathered round a spired church, girt by rolling hills crowned with rich woodland: it could, he decided, have been anywhere in south Oxfordshire.

The weather was fine and exceedingly warm, causing the busy training programme to avoid the midday heat: companies paraded at 7am and worked till 11, and again in the evening from 5 till 7. He found 16 platoon reinvigorated by its time out of the line and was buoyed by its enthusiasm. There was a feeling of unison at last, a common purpose, of moving and behaving as one. The men, even Bostock, responded to his leadership during endless hours of the man-versus-undergrowth manoeuvres that best approximated to warfare in the woods. In the afternoons the men rested, attended classes in the Battalion school organized by Adamson or played cricket, often with Max umpiring.

Max had always distanced himself from the sport most closely associated with the Battalion: boxing. But not this time. A period in rest like this one demanded an inter-company tournament designed to ward off boredom, channel aggression, release anger and fan unit morale. Every officer was expected to participate. Max volunteered as sponge-man.

'Fancy sparrin', sir?' said Bostock, as Max approached the makeshift ring, delineated by a length of rope entwined around four fence posts, where the boxers were training.

Goodey stopped punching a straw-filled flour sack suspended from a tree and began flexing his biceps in the taunting manner of a fairground fighter. 'Come on Mister Lanham! Show us your muscles! I'll spar with you!'

'He's too big for you! A boy's no match for Mister Lanham. 'En't that roight, sir? Goodey's only a featherweight. You'd weigh, what, about twelve-an'-arf?'

Max put down the bucket he was carrying. 'Right on both counts, Bostock.'

'That makes you a nat'ral light-heavy, then.' said Bostock. 'Thass my weight.'

One glance at Bostock's sweat-glistened torso was sufficient to convince Max that every ounce of that weight was hard muscle and that his reputation as the company's undisputed best in that weight division had not come undeserved. Nor could he avoid noticing that Bostock's comments had attracted the attention of the other men in the vicinity. His stomach began to churn.

'Come on, then, Eck!' Goodey called out, ducking under the rope. 'I'll give you a go!'

Bostock ignored Goodey and continued staring at Max. When no response came of his challenge, he rinsed his mouth with a slug of water and spat. 'A'right, short arse. If you got the balls, less be havin' you.'

Goodey dashed from his corner and pranced around the ring. 'Iss Jimmy Wilde, the Might-ee Atom, all the way from Wales! The fly-weight champ-ee-on of the world!' he chanted, his skinny legs skipping furiously and his pipe-stem arms pumping with equal vim.

The men clustered ringside were reduced to hysterics as he bobbed and weaved while throwing lefts and rights that came nowhere within a foot of finding their target. Bostock merely edged from one side to the other like a seasoned pro, his fists cocked, ready to end this farce any time he wanted.

'Hit him with your sucker punch, Arthur!' yelled Dewe. 'He's ready for the takin'. Smack 'im right in the chops!'

Goodey broke off from his flamboyant exhibitionism to smile gormlessly in the direction of Dewe, and promptly received a straight right full in the face. By Bostock's standards the punch only amounted to a pat, but to Goodey it amounted to an exploding grenade that left him flat out on the floor and provoked loud groans from the rest of the platoon.

Goodey raised himself onto all fours and shook his head. And then got up to recommence his attack. Only now his arms flailed rather than jabbed. Bostock swatted them aside and clipped him on the temple as he tottered past. Goodey collapsed in a chest-heaving heap under the rope at Max's feet.

'That's enough, Bostock,' said Max. He knew Bostock had been going easy, the sharpness in his voice more a reflection of knowing who Bostock really wanted inside the ropes. But he was not about to give him the satisfaction.

He hauled Goodey upright and wiped the grass and dirt from his face to reveal his small boy's soft nose and mouth split and bleeding.

'One more round!' shouted Goodey, breaking free and lunging at Bostock.

Bostock let Goodey's flapping arms slide harmlessly over his shoulder and then wrapped his own around Goodey's waist.

'You're a ballsy little bugger!' he said, picking him up as if he were one of Bert Clack's cart-wheels and depositing him on an empty ammunition box Dewe had pushed into the corner. Dewe threw a bucket of water over Goodey and the men cheered at hisinvoluntary impression of a drunk staggering homeward at closing time.

Bostock stood with arms akimbo. 'Reck'n you could do better than that, sir?'

'I'm no boxer,' Max protested, not daring to look Bostock in the eye.

'Neither's Goodey!'

The men laughed and then fell silent. It was that kind of pre-emptive stillness, the religious hush one feels upon waking on a winter's morn knowing without looking that snow lies thick on the ground. It was a silence heavy with intent, a message too obvious for Max to misunderstand. He found himself praying for a convenient way out. And this lack of backbone made him feel ashamed.

'Lads, whad'ya reckon?' said Bostock, surveying the men. 'D'ya think Mister Lanham could handle it?'

'Take no notice of him, sir,' said Dewe. 'He's just spittin' out words to see where they falls.'

'No,' puffed Goodey. 'Go on, sir, knock his blinkin' block off!'

Max remained impassive. On the outside. Inside he felt as if every bad dream that had left him twisting in the sheets had resurfaced as one long nightmare.

Bostock padded to the centre of the ring. 'It's not loik iss the Black Bridge issit?'

He turned his back and permitted himself a broad smile. He had won. Twice over. A new victory to sit beside an old one revived.

He might just get a third because Max had Goodey's gloves in his hands. Leading this rabble into battle was hard enough without knowing every one of them regarded him as a shirker or a gutless wonder.

'Why not!' he said, pulling on the gloves, his resolve fuelled by more logic than courage.

Bostock stopped preening. He flexed his knees and knocked his gloved fists together, and then strode toward Max with the implacability of a hangman attending his scaffold. Arching his neck muscles and rolling his head, a hard glower hammered to his face. He halted an arms-length from Max, and wiggled his boots into the dirt for purchase. The men rushed to the ring and gave a roar of approval.

Pop! Pop! Pop! He jumped into Max, whose guard was still amateurishly low and a trio of left jabs peppered his nose in as many seconds, forcing him to retreat. Bostock chased him, clubbing him with a rabbit punch to the neck and a right uppercut into the ribcage that felt as if it had skewered his liver to his spleen.

Max slumped onto one knee, head bowed as much through reluctance to meet the gaze of his men as the impact of the punches. He ordered himself to display no signs of surrender, though he feared he could not endure such punishment for long. He counted to three and staggered to his feet.

Bostock tore into him. Max covered his face with his gloves and tucked his elbows into his sides in an effort to protect his ribs, and then tried to grab hold of Bostock's waist when he came into close quarters but found it was like trying to hold onto one of Tinegate's buzz-saws. Lefts and rights thudded into his kidneys with a grunting venom gestated over many years. Bostock was relishing the feel of his fists burrowing into Max's soft tissue with such force that the nearest men thought the eyes must pop out of Max's head. But though his mouth dropped open he absorbed them all, his muscles fluttering involuntarily beneath every punch. And with each fresh blow, at first singly and then collectively, his men began cheering him on.

After a flurry of body punches, Bostock paused for breath. Max uncurled himself, and loosed a crude haymaker of a right hand that socked Bostock flush on the jaw and zipped a charge like an electric current to each shoulder blade. Bostock reeled backwards, shaking his head. Once more the men roared. But this time Max knew their approval was for him.

Bostock came back fighting mad. Too mad for a fighting man. Max took most of the wild swings on his arms and backed away into a corner. Bostock poked out a left lead and Max sensed he was being measured up for a knock-out right cross. He remembered something he'd read in a Henty adventure, a trick played by an ageing prizefighter. Once he felt the wooden post at his back he let his hands drop three inches from his face. Bostock saw it and launched a right hook. Max ducked a second after he dropped his guard and heard the whoosh as Bostock's fist whistled over the top of his head and struck the post with a tremendous thwack that very nearly shook it out of the ground.

Bostock's squealed in excruciating pain and sank to the dirt, rolling and clutching his mangled hand. The men winced, feeling every sob of his agony. But they ran to Max and raised his hand.

Max had no energy to celebrate his success or desire to gloat. He quaffed the water Goodey handed him, and offered a silent prayer to God for exercising some divine intervention on his behalf. That and a nod to the power of literature.

Bostock hobbled away cradling his right hand to his chest, his face contorted with pain, a combination of hurt and ignominy that he determined to mete out to Max Lanham whenever he got the chance. He had stolen his girl; his family had lorded it over families like his for too long; every day he was a walking reminder of a well-fed and well-dressed privilege devoid of hard work; and, the worst sin of the lot, he was gutless—he had sensed it in many a ring opponent and he had seen it in the whites of his eyes on the Black Bridge.

Casting aspersions on Max Lanham's manhood by daubing insults on gates may have served its purpose in the past, may have given him some satisfaction back home in sleepy Littlemore, but he was damn sure he could deliver some form of retribution more befitting the hell they presently found themselves inhabiting.

13

Noeux Still

'D'ya have to do that loik you're enjoyin' it?' said Dewe, a look of disgust twisting his face. 'Go an' do you chattin' somewhere else! S'loik watchin' a chimp threadin' a bloomin' needle!'

The platoon was scattered along a grass verge beside the village school, resting backs against the flint-stone wall or stretching out on the grass. Every man had a full stomach. The cooks had provided them with piping hot rissoles made from hard tack soaked and mixed with bully beef before being bound with eggs and rolled in crushed biscuit crumbs and fried in bacon fat. And a pudding of plum duff made from biscuits, sugar and a handful of raisins, steamed and drowned in hot jam sauce. Afterwards a tot of rum was distributed, pipes or cigarettes lit—or in the case of a non-smoker like Goodey, acid drops distributed in lieu of his tobacco ration were sucked instead. 16 platoon, for once, was content. But they all knew what such unaccustomed luxury prefaced.

Goodey continued running a candle along the seams of a pair of long-johns in search of nits, his tongue protruding in concentration, his nose barely an inch from the flame.

'Got no choice! I've already turned this pair inside out once an' the loice are all over me arse again! Counted 85 so far.'

'You can't count that high half-wit!' shouted Bostock, in the act of lighting another cigarette from the stubby embers of the last.

'Your loice must be the fattest in the comp'ny!' moaned Dewe. 'Christ, you're even makin' me itch now!'

'Too bloody big for a midget loik him to crack!' muttered Bostock. He glanced across at Goodey's face wreathed in child-like concentration, picked up the helmet of mucky water that he had just used for shaving and threw it all over him.

'Bloody hell, Bostock! What you playin' at?'

'If you can't crack 'em, might as well drown 'em!'

A guffaw spread from man to man.

'I tell you what,' continued Bostock, 'we could put Steve Donoghue on one of those mickies next time there's some loice races. Bound to win!'

'They say the mobile cinema's due next week,' said Goodey, shaking out his underpants. 'Some proper ent'tainment at last.'

'Fat chance o' that!' observed Dewe, producing a football. 'Who waunts a game? Come on, Littlemore versus Sandford! Gibbo! Chalky! Dodger! Me, Eck and Arthur'll 'ammer you lot of river rats just loik always!'

Gibbons, White and Dodgson bellowed acceptance of the challenge and, after casting away the dregs of their tea and fastening their braces, laid out helmets for goalposts.

'I'm up for it!' shouted Goodey. 'What about you, Eck?'

'Nah. Too bloody full!'

'Come on! You know we can't play without you at the back! Bloomin' brick wall you are! You stops 'em and I bangs 'em in other end!'

Bostock's feigned indifference vanished and he sprang to his feet. 'Oh, a'roight then!'

'Come on the Littlemore lads!' shouted Dewe, hoofing the ball high into the air. Twenty minutes of kick-and-run football ensued, punctuated by the roaring and gesticulating such contests traditionally engendered whether played here or on the Oxford Road pitch back home. When the passion had faded, Dewe, Goodey and Bostock linked arms and victory-jigged off the pitch in a clod-hopping chorus line.

'Who waunts a game o' cards?' said Dewe, collapsing on the ground. 'Brag anyone? Pontoon? Nap?'

Bostock spat into the grass at his feet. 'Nah! You owes me arf a million quid a'ready!'

'We could play for real money?'

'Piss off!'

'We've just bin paid!' protested Dewe.

'Yes, an' I'm keepin' moine!'

'Next trip to Ma Cholley's?' piped up Goodey, wiping the sweat off his forearms. 'Some decent bints there!'

'And what would a Johnny-no-dick like you know 'bout the bints at Ma Cholley's?'

'Back home I got . . .'

'Bollocks! Got a right hand, thass all!' sneered Bostock. 'Stick to sendin' lacy postcards to your mother!'

Goodey blushed, and placed his hand over the pink-edged card poking out of his tunic pocket.

'Home!' grunted Dewe. 'Shut-up about home! I can't be thinkin' about those bastards havin' it cushy back 'ome.'

'Sorry, Sam,' said Goodey, pushing the latest postcard to his mother out of sight.

Dewe rammed his heel into the grass until he'd excavated a divot. 'I heard they can get 70 shillings a week makin' shells in a nice comfy fact'ry! Seventy bloomin' shillins a week! An' I got a poxy 16 on the farm for breakin' me back all week!'

He stopped stroking the platoon's pet cat and tossed it aside. 'And over here we gets 12 bob for loik as not gettin' our arses shot off!'

'Now you'll have summut else to bellyache about!' interjected Corporal Fenn, who had just arrived and overheard the end of the conversation. 'Mister Lanham wants the entire platoon up on that ridge yonder . . .'

'What for?' squealed Goodey.

'Someone's got to fell some trees and dig some pits ready for gun emplacements . . .'

'Manual bloody labour!' Bostock shouted, jumping to his feet. 'Let the bloody Canucks do it! They're always crowin' they're bleedin' lumberjacks! We're in a rest area for Chrissake!'

'Christ don't have no say in it, and before you get on his back neither did Mister Lanham. So, come on, let's be 'aving you!'

The men were reluctant to move. These quiet moments were sacrosanct. It was their only chance of some daily respite from the trappings of war. A window of time when they could be more like the men who worked and played together back home. Belts were buckled but slowly and tobacco juice spat onto the ground in silent contempt.

Once he had finally succeeded in rousing them, Fenn led 16 platoon at a wheezing saunter up to the wood-clad ridge where their officer and a truck laden with saws, axes, picks and shovels was waiting for them in the welcome shade.

'Gentlemen,' said Max, cheerfully. 'Grab your weapon of choice and let's get started.'

Max was unsure if cheerfulness was in order. He knew how the men would feel about this additional chore. His own peaceful afternoon had been disrupted and Yeats cast aside. But it seemed preferable to replicating their truculence.

Bostock seized a pick and lent on it; those slower on the uptake were left with the axes and saws. Goodey drew a heavy two-man saw. Max noticed the smirk on Bostock's face.

'Bostock, we can't have those blacksmith's muscles of yours going to waste,' he said with a new-found cockiness the men had been pleased to note in him since his fight with Bostock. 'Swap that pick for an axe and get cracking on that tree over there.'

The men grinned. Bostock scowled.

Max unbuckled his Sam Browne. 'Goodey, you look as if you could do with some help. Here, I'll take the other end.'

'Sir . . . you can't do that.'

'Rubbish! I'm not about to stand around watching you lot all afternoon.'

Max allocated trees to the rest of the working party while he and Goodey started on the nearest, a small beech. They quickly established a zizzing rhythm and began smiling at each other as they increased the tempo, totally engaged in an impossible race to see which of them could finish first.

'Beggars belief, eh Goodey? Hardly a tree around here that's not been blown to kingdom come and here we are chopping down the survivors!'

They retreated to watch the beech crash and bounce to earth; Max beckoned Gibbons and Pitson forward to remove the stump and roots with pick and shovel.

Max and Goodey switched their attention to the adjacent tree, which they scanned from top to bottom with the air of experienced foresters. Max took a fresh grip on his end of the saw, but Goodey continued to stare up into the top-most branches.

'Come on, Goodey! Shift yourself!'

'But sir, there's a nest up there!'

'What?'

'There's a bird in it! I can see the 'ead movin'. She must be sittin' on summut or she'd have scarpered be-now.'

Goodey leapt onto the trunk like a squirrel and began ascending as if he were bringing home the winter nuts. 'Only be a tick, sir! Might be able to move her somewhere safer.'

Max shook his head, wiped his brow and walked over to sit on the trunk of the fallen beech. He watched Goodey edge along the branch and saw the bird, a greenfinch he thought, flap off the nest.

'Only eggs!' Goodey called down.

'Then get back down here!'

Max was returning his handkerchief to his pocket when the sound of cracking twigs and a cry of 'Shit!' made him look up: Goodey was dangling from the branch, desperately swinging his legs up and down in an effort to throw one over the branch and save himself from falling.

Goodey's predicament attracted the attention of the other men who instinctively succumbed to making monkey noises.

'For Christ's sake, man!' shouted Max. 'Stop fooling about! I'll throw you a rope!'

'S'all right, sir! Iss only six or seven foot or so. I'll drop down!'

'Goodey, don't be so bloody stupid!'

'Let him jump!' called Bostock, squatting on an axe handle shoved between his legs. 'Might land on summut soft. Like his bleedin' head!'

Max glowered at Bostock as he ran to the truck, but before he laid a hand on the rope he was knocked off his feet by an explosion.

Every man in the wood dived for cover, waiting for a second shell to arrive. Ten seconds passed. Then another ten. No more shelling. The men started to call out to each other. Max felt as if an invisible giant had struck him in the small of the back with a hammer. He searched for the sticky evidence of a wound; but feeling only grubby fingers he struggled to his feet.

The dust cloud drifted away, and he saw Goodey lying on his back near what remained of the tree. Max staggered across to him and immediately sank to the ground, covering his mouth.

'Sir, let me take a dekko,' said Dewe. He took one look and burst into tears, huge manful dollops, his face a map of grief. 'Jesus Christ Almighty! What have they done to him?'

Goodey's upper body was unmarked, but he had been practically severed at the midriff by a huge hole; his hands seemed to be fumbling for his right leg or else trying to contain his intestines which had spilled out across his hips like sausages on a butcher's slab. It was the best Goodey could manage for though his mind still worked it was in slow motion. He thought he'd watched the bird fly away, and now he thought he saw some vaguely familiar faces leaning over him. He hoped he'd caught his ticket home, his 'Blighty' wound. But he could see the blood pumping out of him, and it was starting to hurt. He feared he'd bought it good and proper.

'Am I gunner die, sir?' he mumbled.

'Die?' Max replied, caught in the spotlight of Goodey's thousand-yard stare.

'Good Lord, no!' he added. 'We'll get you back and patched up in a jiffy. You'll be right as rain.'

Goodey fought back the tears. 'Thank you, sir.'

Max brushed the dirt from Goodey's cheeks and gently thumbed away spots of blood that had stuck to the few scattered hairs on his chin. 'That's quite a beard you're cultivating . . . just rest easy, and think about showing it off to your mother when you get home on leave.'

He looked down into eyes resembling two of Mrs Tedder's poached eggs and watched them close.

Behind them Goodey was wondering why Mister Lanham hadn't answered him; he'd always found time to chat in the past. He tried to ask if it was his fault, if he'd done something wrong or caused offence. But although he felt his lips moving he could hear no sound.

Max cradled his head and smoothed the matted hair off his forehead, longing for his friend's suffering to end. He wanted to reassure him but his mouth was as dusty as the white chalk dirt caking his face like a *pierrot*'s makeup: and he could not find the right words because there were none. Goodey's lifeblood was gushing out of him in a frothy scarlet stream.

'Thass a proper 25 bob a week job!' said Bostock. 'I reck'n you can call that full disablement a'roight.'

Dewe shrieked and lunged at him with his shovel. 'You're a mean bastard Bostock! I'll put a bayonet in your guts one o' these days!'

Bostock dodged the shovel and buried a fist into Dewe's stomach, knocking him to the ground.

'Corporal Fenn!' Max shouted. 'Take the men away from here. There's nothing they can do!'

'Yes sir. I've sent for stretcher bearers . . .'

'No bloody need for 'em!' sniggered Bostock. 'Bloody shovel'll do the job!'

Bostock leant back on the tree stump, and was struck on the head by something dislodged from one of the few surviving branches.

'Shit! It's his bleedin' leg!' he screamed, kicking the limb away. 'Got the soddin' boot on an all!'

'Get that bloody man out of my sight!' Max yelled. 'Or I'll put a bayonet through him myself!'

Max turned away. 'And throw a tunic over this man!'

The half-arsed grin faded from Bostock's face once he saw that no one else was sharing his amusement. Not one man wanted to look him in the eye. They knew he was shamming. They loathed his outburst just like Dewe and Max, but they understood what had driven it because the same thought had occurred to each of them: the platoon was due a casualty and if Goodey was that casualty it meant it could not be one of them.

They shuffled away, leaving Max sitting in a lake of blood, holding Goodey's wrecked body and staring into blank eyes that, unbeknownst to him, were presenting the stricken soldier with the solace of a friendly face at the moment of death.

Max felt life's warmth steadily ebbing out of his friend. But it took five minutes before Goodey's pallid lips stopped moving. He wanted to know where everyone had gone and what they would all be doing tomorrow. He had no idea no one was listening and he would never get to know the answers. He died wondering about what the future held for him—just as he had spent most of his life.

Max lowered the dead man's eyelids and waited for the stretcher bearers while birdsong once again began filling the trees around him and he got to thinking how much longer he could endure this madness.

'Sleep well, Arthur,' he whispered. 'You're out of it now.'

14

Ma Cholley's

They buried Goodey the following morning. The wrist-jarring chalk prevented them from digging a grave any deeper than three feet, which they marked with a crude wooden cross and Goodey's helmet. Making the effort was what mattered to Max, for he was aware his friend's resting place would soon be churned up by shells and all trace of Arthur Goodey wiped from the face of the earth. Max patted the blanketed corpse as it was lowered into the ground and afterwards led the Lord's Prayer with an audible crack in his voice.

They reckoned that when Goodey jumped out of the tree he must have landed on a buried or booby-trapped grenade, a favourite Hun trick. Max wrote to Goodey's parents, trotting out the usual guff about the deceased 'feeling no pain . . . death was instantaneous . . . a much valued member of the platoon . . . respected by all his comrades.' He committed the lies to paper picturing the desolation on those two familiar faces as they tried coming to terms with their grief, and felt a total fraud when he finally put his name to the deception.

And Max had one more deception to progress before his day was done. Any honourable intentions to speak with Peter Revell about his affection for Rowan Hawes had been sidelined by Revell attending an anti-gas seminar at GHQ. Revell was due back that evening and Max had arranged to dine with him in Noeux's town hall which now served as the officers mess.

The two officers greeted each other with a handshake that typified their relationship: firmer than mere acquaintance but not so strong as outright friendship. They had enjoyed a brief period at school where it had approached the latter, but Revell's premature departure ended any such consummation. Max eyed him from his shiny pips to his buffed boots and appreciated why joining the Army had been a wise decision for him and a dim one for himself.

'Good to see you, Max! All the better for a spot of Blighty, eh?'

The smile was wide and genuine, the kind that reassured his superiors and charmed his female relatives.

'I can't complain,' replied Max. 'But after yesterday's mishap I wish I'd stayed longer.'

Revell's long thin face narrowed until his eyes seemed to touch. 'Yes, I heard. Nasty business.'

'Buried grenade. Known the boy all my life. And his parents. God knows how they are going to cope. Only son, you see . . .'

Max's voice tailed off like a dud note on a piano.

'Just like us two,' observed Revell, clapping Max on the back. 'Let's tie on the nosebag, shall we? Shan't get too many chances of decent fodder where we're going.'

Max raised his eyebrows. 'You heard something at GHQ then?'

'Pretty common knowledge that there's big stunt in the offing . . .'

'Hence all this training?'

'Yes,' drawled Revell, 'though it's disappointing to read about it first in the newspapers they send us rather than hear it from the top brass.'

'The *Daily Mail* is full of it,' confirmed Max.

'And GHQ is unhappy with Harmsworth, I can tell you,' added Revell, dropping his voice and tapping his nose as he invited Max to take a seat.

Max leant across the table. 'Peter, are we going into the front line?'

'We are indeed, orders for the whole of the 184th Brigade to move north will be issued tomorrow. After we've eaten it might be a capital idea to motor down to Amiens, have a night at Charley's Bar before things get rough. What do you say?'

'Sounds all right for the likes of me, but you?' asked Max, barely concealing his astonishment that Revell should contemplate a visit to

Amien's most notorious *maison close* devoted to sensual pleasure. 'What about Rowan Hawes?'

'What she doesn't know won't do her any harm, will it? And where else am I going to get my end away before the push? I'm not using the blue-light in Noeux!'

Max nodded: the 'approved' brothels—the *maisons tolerates*— designated for officers only (as opposed to the red-light variety for other ranks) held no appeal for him either after his first encounter with an 'approved' tart left him with crabs. Nor could he dispute the veracity of a soldier's sexual appetite veering toward a state of frenzy when an offensive was looming.

'Those girls at Charley's cost a week's pay!' he ventured.

'I've a stash of chocolate, champagne and cigarettes to sweeten them up,' countered Revell. 'They know me. We'll not be overcharged.'

Max began slicing the beef placed before him and smiled at this cavalier indication of Revell's shallow affection for Rowan Hawes: it filled him with joy.

'I can see you're warming to the idea,' said Revell, pointing his knife accusingly. 'Speaking of the devil, how was Rowan? Did you visit? Probably too busy I imagine? Never mind.'

All of a sudden Max felt no compulsion to behave honourably. 'Actually, I did pay her a visit.'

'Is that so?'

'She is very well. And I put her mind at rest, as you asked. Delightful girl.'

'I think so,' said Revell, before popping a potato into his mouth.

'And you're to be married?'

Revell took an age chewing and swallowing the potato before deigning to answer 'I think so.'

'You don't sound very sure, Peter.'

'Seems pretty much set for standing orders but I don't know whether she's cut out to be an Army wife.'

'In what way?'

Revell placed knife and fork neatly on his plate and swept his mouth with his napkin. 'Bit headstrong sometimes. Spiky . . . if you know what I mean . . .'

'Disobeys orders?' Max said behind a sly grin.

'Yes! Good way of putting it!'

Max looked at Revell's chuckling face and felt like telling him he was a fool. Furthermore, if that was how he felt about Rowan Hawes then he would not care two hoots if another were to offer her the love she deserved. And that he, Max Lanham, would marry her instead. That's what Max felt like saying. As it was, he said nothing and silently thanked the Lord.

'She's fought her way up from nowhere. Parents run a general store. But she had something! They found her in the shop reading *The Times* when she was only six! Studied all hours. Sailed through the Higher Certificate and won a bursary to Royal Holloway College to study English Lit. Then her father died suddenly. There was no money to pay her tuition fees, so she gave up her place and went home to help her mother run the shop.'

Max fought to keep his mouth closed as his brain absorbed all this telling information. 'She never said . . .'

'No, she wouldn't. Not her style. Kept studying in her spare time, of course, and became a governess. One of her chums told me that her tutors at the Royal Holloway were convinced she was on for a First.'

'Perhaps she'll return to college one day . . .'

'Doubt it. Energies go elsewhere . . . I suspect she's in cahoots with those bloody suffragettes!'

Max took his turn to smile. He should've guessed.

Revell downed the last of his red wine. 'I shall have to tame her!'

'Some birds are too beautiful to cage,' responded Max quickly—perhaps too quickly he thought once the words had left his lips.

Revell noticed the distant look in his companion's eyes, but attached little significance to it: Lanham had always been an odd cove in school and tales of his unorthodoxy over here merely endorsed the view.

'I don't think I'll take up your offer, Peter,' said Max, getting to his feet. 'Thanks all the same.'

'As you wish,' Revell replied in a voice high with surprise. 'Then I'll see you anon.'

The two officers parted at the door and while Revell drove off into the western sky, Max walked in the other direction toward the twinkling red light of Madame Cholley's.

Ma's place was meant to be an *estaminet*, a small café or bar where a soldier might relax over a one-franc bottle of wine (sweetened with sugar to suit English taste buds) bolt down a plate of home-cooked egg and chips or just sing along to the accordion player. Ma's offered additional services, however: outside the door snaked a queue of Tommies eager to take their turn with one of her girls in exchange for five francs.

The sexually-charged banter subsided at the sight of an officer. Then a lone voice rang out: 'Comin' to join us, sir? Oh, it's only Mister Lanham! Goin' home for his cocoa, I 'spect!'

The men roared with laughter at Bostock's ribaldry before fighting to get inside and preserve their anonymity. Max halted, cracked his swagger stick against his boot and marched across the road. Sergeant Clinkard's words echoed inside his skull, but not for the first time he ignored them: no one was going to have a laugh at his expense. Least ofall Hector-bloody-Bostock.

Max entered an establishment decked out pleasantly with coloured lights and artificial flowers. Yet the overpowering sensations were its heat, its smoke, its noise and, it pained Max to admit, its unbridled gaiety. The latter clearly derived from two factors: drink and loose woman. Every table was littered with bottles, beer bottles and wine bottles: the lamps shining through the wine bottles demonstrated one way Ma Cholley made her money for the, so-called, full bottles were in fact only two-thirds full. Most of the clientele were already too drunk or too preoccupied with ogling the serving girls who, flowers tucked into their hair, weaved effortlessly between the tables while managing to balance trays of food and drink with the dexterity of a plate-spinning act in circus. He couldn't help noticing that they seemed to be wearing nothing under their dresses. Indeed, it would have been impossible not to because they seized any opportunity to fondle their breasts under the noses of the troops when bending down to deposit plates of food or else lift their hems in a mock can-can when empty-handed.

Ma Cholley oversaw her operation from a *chaise longue* on a raised dais in the corner. Tall and thin, but with a pronounced pot-belly, she wore far too much rouge and orange powder which, thanks to the peacock feather stuck in her hair, made her resemble a redskin squaw.

'Officer-boy!' she cooed when she noticed the pips on his shoulder. 'You want Ma to come upstairs with you?'

Her fat-lips curled into a scowl as Max ignored her. 'Too much woman for a boy, eh!'

She watched him pass and the scowl altered to a smirk. 'Ma has pills that will make you strong!'

Max didn't hear a word. Ma's six-year-old daughter jumped off the end of the *chaise longue* and pursued him, clinging to his breeches while begging for chocolate, as he searched the tables and corners for Bostock.

The room erupted into a lusty rendition of *Inky Pinky Parleyvoo*, Goodey's song.

> *Far-mer 'ave yer a door-ter fine?*
> *Par-lee-voo!*

Bang-bang went their feet against the stone floor.

> *Far-mer 'ave yer a door-ter fine?*
> *Par-lee-voo!*

Another thumping bang-bang.

> *Far-mer 'ave yer a door-ter fine?*
> *Fit for a sol-jer up the line?*
> *Ink-ee Pink-ee Par-lee-voo!*

The final chorus was drowned by an even louder, table-rocking bang-bang accompanied by a raucous assortment of 'Whorrs and Drop-yer-drawers-the-money's-yours!'

Max heard Goodey's squeaky tenor echoing in his brain. He felt the after-taste of roast beef rise in his craw, and began pushing men aside to reach the staircase. Bostock, he guessed, must be upstairs. He reached the landing where the men sat on benches opposite the row of bedrooms, all the speedier to select their girl of choice when she became available.

'Well, I en't havin' the big bint with the fat legs!' Dewe was saying.

'What about Pug?' slurred Pitson. 'She may have a flat 'ooter but she bangs loik a shithouse door! And thass what matters, dunnit?'

Gibbons was unmoved, staring trance-like at the ceiling. 'I'm waitin' for Vicki! Juss thinkin' 'bout those long legs of hers in that teeny schoolgirl skirt. Loik bloody nutcrackers they are! An' black hair tied back with that satin bow . . . it's enough to make me splash me pants!'

The three of them began stamping their feet in unison until dust spiralled like Apache smoke signals from between the floorboards.

'You'll 'ave a long wait!' Dewe said. 'Hector'll waunt to take his time with 'er!'

Gibbons shrugged, and then pointed to a poster on the wall. 'What wouldn't I give for ten minutes on top o' one loik that while I'm waitin' for Eck to drop his load!'

Max followed their eyes to the poster which advertised a French beer. It depicted a titian-haired girl with green eyes, head angled back in laughter, sporting a come-hither smile that left men like his in no doubt as to the true nature of her invitation.

Their officer began grinding his teeth. All Max saw smiling out from the poster was Rowan Hawes. And it churned his guts: with both yearning and revulsion. That common soldiers might leer at a woman like her, desire her just as much as he did, made her appear unclean and him feel depraved.

'Good God!' he shouted, quivering with rage. 'Look at you! Behaving like scum and not 24 hours after burying one of your own!'

The men fell silent, immune to the bacchanalia around them. Their officer had broken one of first laws of trench life.

'It's the only way to forget, sir,' said Dewe quietly.

'But how can you think of women like they were sex objects?'

'Beggin' your pardon, sir,' said Dewe, 'But this en't 'xactly a nunnery, an' these certainly en't nuns! An' why do we get these handed to us if you don't waunt us to indulge ourselves?'

Max took the postcard Dewe was holding out to him and examined it. It showed a soldier bending a half-naked woman backward over a bed.

'Dewe, you're a moron! Have you not noticed the soldier is wearing a German uniform? This is a propaganda card designed to fill you with horror and hate for the enemy not act as some sort of pornographic inducement.'

'Oops!' said Dewe. And the rest mimicked likewise.

'Have you no respect?' Max fumed. 'Have none of you mothers? Have none of you sisters?'

'Not loik that!'

The voice was Bostock's. He stood in a bedroom doorway with his arm draped around Vicki's shoulders.

'Oh, yes, I can see the loikness, sir,' he said, advancing toward the poster and patting the girl's bosom. 'Bet you'd love to get your 'ands on one loik this, eh sir?'

Max blinked furiously, fists clenched by his side.

'News gets around. Me brother told me in his last letter,' said Bostock, now fondling Vicki's breast. 'Caught you down the river, didn't ee?'

The men sniggered.

Max could have been a granite obelisk for all the vitality he had in him. Bostock had blind-sided him and he had no idea how best to retaliate. He wanted to hit him; but he couldn't hit him. For once, a sharp-tongued put-down would not come. His head was spinning. What was he doing in here at all? Why didn't he follow Clinkard's wise counsel? Why couldn't he have accepted Revell's invitation?

'Get back to your billets!' he shouted at length. 'Tomorrow you're heading north to . . .'

Every man held his breath and every head turned his way.

'. . . Ypres.'

Max sensed the old hands saying their prayers under their breath and felt pleasure at their pain as if it were some kind of retribution for the slight they had just paid Rowan Hawes—and the pain they had caused him.

'No, not bloody Wipers!' Dewe moaned, dropping his head.

'Corr, thass Belgium, en't it?' said Gibbons. 'En't never bin to Belgium!'

'Shut up, numbskull. You'll soon wish you 'adn't!' muttered Bostock.

They walked out into a gloom giving the impression someone had dropped a black cloth over the setting sun. The sky to the west was low and dark, full to overflowing with menace. It began to spit with rain. By the time they reached their billets it had turned to drizzle. And while they twitched in their beds scratching their lice and thinking of Ypres the drizzle turned into heavy rain.

The rain would not stop for four days. The Third Battle of Ypres would be fought in a quagmire.

15

To Vlamertinghe

The following morning the Battalion began its trek north, by train to St Omer and then on foot, to camp around the scattered hamlet of Broxeele for further training.

The training in question was gas drill. Max had a week to educate his men in the theory and practice of taking immediate counter-measures whenever the gas warning was shouted or the gas alarm honked. For once he had the immediate and rapt attention of 16 platoon.

If there was one weapon the men feared more than artillery it was gas. At least being blown to bits by a shell was quick. Gas could inflict a horrible, lingering, agonizing death. Every man had heard the stories even if he had not had the misfortune to come across a victim in the field: sufferers gradually being eaten away inside and out by burns, not bearing to be bandaged or touched, gasping for breath from congested and slow—roasting lungs, begging for death.

The men listened as Max used a blackboard to spell out the dangers of the latest gas being used by the enemy. After experimenting with chlorine and phosgene the Germans were now using mustard gas. An oily brown liquid that looked like sherry and smelt of onions, garlic or radishes, it was dispatched in shells and the gas released on detonation; if there was no sunlight or the soil was dry the liquid evaporated slowly and might seep into the earth, contaminate water or cling to the churned soil for days, quite capable of burning and blistering anything

143

that came into contact. Direct contact caused moist red patches, like scarlet fever blemishes, that blistered inside 24 hours—even nurses who treated the casualties often developed coughs and saw their hair turn yellow. The effects of exposure were not felt for two or three hours, whereupon sneezing set in and copious mucous, like the onset of flu, developed. Meanwhile the eyelids swelled, throats burned, heads ached and eventually the mucous membranes in the lungs and liver collapsed. In the worst cases, even the genitals were lost.

The men exchanged glances; no more. Not one stirred as Max chalked up his final statistic in bold capital letters and read it aloud: 'The average man has 3000 square inches of skin for the vapour to attack. So protect it. Listen and obey.'

He told them they must not drink water from shell-holes in any sector that had received gas or sit on anything that resembled a used shell. They must use their sense of smell—however difficult it seemed to detect one particular odour among the many that proliferated on a battlefield—and that, above all, they must always carry their gas masks and be prepared to put them on hastily.

Max reached into a canvas bag and pulled out an ugly-looking contraption that instantly provoked griping chatter.

'Quiet! This is a box respirator, the latest type of gas mask which will be issued tomorrow for drilling under pressure conditions. There's a clip here that goes on your nose and this canister here contains charcoal and other chemicals which neutralizes the gas and connects by tube to the face mask and its breathing valves. These eye-pieces protect your eyes.'

Max pulled the face mask over his head and the men broke into raucous laughter.

'I'm not wearin' that!' shouted Bostock. 'Looks loik a goggle-eyed frog with a tit! Rather take me chances pissing onto me bloody handkerchief an' usin' that!'

The men cheered.

'Your choice in the end, Bostock!' said Max. 'But tomorrow you'll start learning how to put it on in six seconds! And that goes for all of you!'

Bostock's proficiency was bound to be tested when, prior to entraining for Poperinghe, the Battalion was inspected by the Corps Commander, General Hunter Weston. Even so, everyone was caught unawares when it was the General himself who suddenly bellowed 'Gas!' while routinely examining rifles and mess tins.

Amid the pandemonium a shot rang out. One of 16 platoon had dropped his rifle and accidentally discharged a round.

Adamson barked: 'Find that man and put him on report!' Max could not: no one was prepared to own up. Rifles should've been cleaned and empty. The slovenly soldier would undoubtedly receive Field Punishment. Max gave the culprit one final opportunity to declare himself, or else he threatened to volunteer someone himself. He hoped silence would continue to prevail because he had a name in mind. After a judicious delay, he called: 'Bostock! CO's report!'

Bostock got ten days Number One Field Punishment: Max tried hard not to smile as he watched Clinkard strap Bostock by ankles and wrists to the muddiest wheel of the muckiest wagon for two hours a day, one in the morning and one in the afternoon. In itself the punishment was no hardship but it demeaned a man to be made to look a fool: which had been Max's intention and which, to his delight, the snarl disfiguring Bostock's face and the grins sported by the remainder of 16 platoon, only served to confirm. Max made a point of halting every time he passed the shackled Bostock and permitting the faintest of smiles to illuminate his face. At first he was met with defiance, but after three days Bostock began staring at the ground as soon as he saw his officer approaching. Max responded by breaking into a whistle.

The Battalion moved forward to Poperinghe on 14 August, a fortnight after the Third Battle of Ypres had commenced. Max found the town degenerate-looking, by a few towers rendered impressive from the approaching train but the reality proving otherwise, many of the buildings they passed leaving the station having suffered considerable damage from long-range German guns. The men's marching did grow more enthusiastic as they entered the high brick-walled yard of an ancient brewery: until they noticed the smile on Max's face and heard him shout 'Clothes off!' This was no surprise reward from the top brass: the brewery had been converted into a de-lousing station.

The men stripped off, constructing neat bundles of their uniform, boots and helmets and tossing their underclothes into a separate pile that was bound for the fumigator. They filed into the building where three huge vats were connected by planks laid in between. The first vat was full of hot water, now conspicuously dirty and soap-scummed.

Each man dropped into the water and pulled himself to the other side by an overhanging rope before negotiating the plank into the second vat that contained slightly less dirty hot water to rinse himself off. The third and final vat contained clean, but cold, water. Towels and a fresh set of underclothes awaited them at the far end of the building.

'These buggers never fit!' moaned Dewe as he struggled to pull his long-johns over his stomach. 'This pair's gone roight up me arse! Bloody cut me in arf, they will!'

The theatricality and self-deprecation rapidly diminished. De-lousing and fresh underclothes meant the ghastly inevitable was edging closer. As did the increasingly common sight of dead horses, lying pathetically bloated and stinking where they fell. So too the continual thunder of the guns and their flashes that lit up the night skies. They would soon be going into the line.

Four days later the Battalion set off on foot for the chateau at Rossieres, half-a-mile from Ypres, known to the troops as 'Goldfish' Chateau, where it would bivouac and await orders. The latest replacements watched the old lags rub wet soap on their feet before donning two pairs of socks, and followed suit. Even those precautions seldom guaranteed a trouble-free march. Each man was laden with between 55 and 80lb of equipment, comprising rifle, haversack, gas-mask, water bottle, Mills bombs, ammunition and entrenching tools. Down the back of every fourth man was the 'unlucky' pickaxe or shovel that sent him into battle ramrod-straight, unable to crouch or dodge bullets. They marched four abreast, whistling and singing, counting the kilometres, wishing them away, but if their progress was not hampered by being forced to circumvent shell-holes or leap out of the path of a swaying limber coming the other way, it was plagued by the interminable cobblestones. Blisters or sore feet or 'footsloggers nodule', the thick nodules of skin that came from the pressure of bootlaces on tendons, or possibly even all three, awaited the unfortunate by day's end.

The terrain they traversed was flat and uninteresting to men accustomed to rolling hills and picturesque valleys: it amounted to bog-land, reclaimed from the sea, that was only prevented from returning to its natural sogginess by a patchwork of drainage ditches. But being unable to penetrate the heavy clay topsoil, the biblical downpours of late had waterlogged the surface and transformed it into a morass; and wherever shelling had destroyed the ditch walls or excavated a crater the men saw vast lakes of brown sludge occasionally dotted with denuded tree trunks that reminded them of candles on a chocolate birthday cake.

Approaching Vlamertinghe they passed a battery readying six-inch howitzers and sang even louder at the prospect of their 26 cwt shells pounding the Hun as far as six miles distant. The spring brought to their step was soon negated by the awful realization that this proved the front line was getting painfully close. They smartened up entering the town in response to an energetic welcome from the regimental band, and further still when they smelt the field kitchens, mounted on two limbers, belching the savoury steam from a bully beef stew that had been simmering away all morning in anticipation of their arrival.

They filled their mess tins with stew and their mugs with steaming tea, and sat down to enjoy their final hot meal before combat in the eerie surroundings of a cemetery. A smattering of intact gravestones gave backrests to a lucky few, but for the majority there was no comfort. Nor, more importantly, any cover.

'An omen, or what?' said Dewe, leaning his rifle against the remains of a once grand tomb before wiggling his backside on top of it.

'This place scares the shit out o' me!' muttered Gibbons.

They set to chomping and slurping, each locked in the haven of his own mind. Thinking of home; the bacon clanger their mother's cooked; a pint of Morrells bitter at The George; the warm responsive body of a Littlemore girl.

There was no warning. No time for a man to compose himself. Suddenly a noise like a freight train rent the air. A fraction later the train smashed into the buffers. Then a second train. And then a third shell speared into the ground.

Men began screaming as if they'd seen the ghosts of their forefathers. Bodies rained down on them. Not raw corpses dripping blood but fetid bodies ripped from the earth. The cemetery had begun to give up its dead. Bodies wrapped in shrouds; bodies hanging from splintered coffins.

Dewe and Bostock instinctively rolled into the first shell hole, praying the old soldier's maxim of no two shells ever landing on the same spot was true. They found themselves sharing the hole with decomposing corpses more slime than flesh. Gibbons slid in after them, and immediately threw up.

Another train approached. 'Shit!' yelled Bostock. 'That sounds bloody close!'

They heard the shell coming straight for them and frantically tried to dig themselves into the mire as if it might offer some hope of escaping being blown to smithereens. Then there was a thud and silence.

'Christ!' said Dewe, looking up at the shell sticking out of the ground beside their hole. 'A bleedin dud!'

Bostock lay on his back, panting. 'If Jerry had my number on that bastard it wuz the wrong bleedin' number!'

'Let's get out o' here!'

'Don't be daft! This is a lucky 'ole. I'm stayin' put! You get yourself blown to bits if you waunts. I'm tellin' you, this 'ole is a bleedin' lucky one!'

Shells continued to fall as though every German gun within six miles was trained on their tiny patch of ground. The screams and shouting rose with every shell.

'Will somebody shoot that bloody horse!' he yelled between salvos. 'Poor bugger!'

Dewe had worked with horses all his life and never thought them capable of screaming—until now. Their pathetic cries joined the moans of men similarly maimed to produce a duet more harrowing than the shelling itself; an ordeal as excruciating as having a drill relentlessly grinding away on a wisdom tooth without the succour of novocaine.

Gibbons began crying. 'Mum! Oh Mum!'

Bostock put his mouth directly to Gibbons's ear to make himself heard. 'Shut up, fer Chrissake!'

Gibbons tore at his collar, fighting to release the terror that had taken control of him, and wailed even louder.

'Shut him up! He's givin' me the willies!' snarled Bostock. 'Or else put a bullet in 'im!'

'Be fair, Eck! It's Gibbo's first shellin''

'It'll be his bloody last an' all!'

Dewe grabbed Gibbons by the throat with one hand, and slapped his face hard with the other. 'Belt up! If Lanham cops you bawlin' loik a woman you'll be done for cowardice.'

Dewe slapped him again even harder. 'D'ya waunt that? D'ya wauner be shot?'

Gibbons slumped lifelessly into Dewe's arms and lay there, grizzling.

The barrage lasted 20 minutes, and when it ceased Max found the pair of them asleep in the shell hole, arms wrapped around each other, covered in mud and guts. But alive. It had been a 'lucky' hole. Dodgeson and White were dead; Fenn had lost an arm to shrapnel, nasty but he'd survive. It was a 'Blighty' wound. Max was pleased for him; he had been a reliable soldier and was a sound man to have around. Fenn would be missed.

His attention was diverted by the sight of Bostock wandering around the cemetery, a string of boots slung around his neck and a haversack in each hand into which he was stuffing every article of value he could find. Why, thought Max, did it have to be White and Dodgeson who copped it and not Bostock.

'Looting again, eh?' said Max. 'Is nowhere sacred to scavengers like you?'

Bostock sniffed. 'It may be scavengin' to you, but this stuff's currency to us.'

'Dead men's bones?'

'No, watches, medals, coins . . .'

'They belong to the next of kin . . .'

Bostock laughed. 'Not these, they don't! These came up when the graves blew Juss now! You'd be surprised what they had buried with 'em.'

'And that makes it all right?' fumed Max. 'It's grave-robbing!'

'I don't think they waunts 'em any more, an' I can't hear any complainin'.

Max had no retort. His eyes teared as he surveyed the carnage surrounding him. He wondered what manner of men he commanded as he watched Bostock walk away whistling contentedly. Or was it a case of decent men being corrupted by the sheer relentless horror of war. In many instances, perhaps. In the person of Bostock he was less sure. Why couldn't he have been reduced to pulp instead of poor Dodgeson and White?

For no reason Max immediately fathomed, he found his right hand straying toward his holster.

16

Pond Farm

Fanned by a rising wind, the night air grew colder. So bitter that Max wondered if snow was in the air in spite of it being only late August.

He and Revell lay in their fleabags in a smoke-filled dugout, handkerchiefs protecting their faces from the black fumes belching from an old coke brazier, fully-clothed bar boots and tunics yet warmed only by their dreams. Their cave measured five paces square and about six feet high and lay at the end of a 15-feet shaft burrowed into the side of a trench. The walls owed their solidity to wooden beams and wire netting, while the roof was a sheet of corrugated iron on top of which sat a foot of earth, enough to withstand a direct mortar hit—but not a six-inch shell. Their tunics and greatcoats lay across two green camp chairs; gumboots and rifle magazines littered the floor.

Neither man could sleep for coughing, and they took turns to desert the warmth of their sleeping bags to rub hands before their tub of warmth and then wind up the portable gramophone that Revell had brought back with him from his last leave. The fact that he only brought two records, and one of those soon broken, was never allowed to destroy the air of escapism fanned by humming along with *Keep the Home Fires Burning*.

They had eaten supper some hours ago. Canisters had been brought up containing meat and vegetables and stewed apples, which they rounded off with coffee brewed on the brazier and laced with rum.

151

They ate in silence and then tried to snatch forty winks, each alone with his thoughts. Had they known they were both thinking of the woman whose letters were tucked into their shirt pockets the situation may have been untenable.

Max had still not made a clean breast of it. He hoped Rowan Hawes would take the responsibility from him but unless Revell was the most forgiving man in Christendom his equanimity suggested she had not.

Her letters to Max steered clear of the subject. His spirits soared every time he saw her flowing handwriting on an envelope, but he received fewer than he wrote and the feeling of possible rejection this triggered in him was underscored by their contents avoiding any mention of her feelings toward him. They were exquisitely crafted pieces of storytelling—a world apart from a child-like note scrawled on the page of an exercise book that he received from Chick or the mundane letters from his mother forever telling him to 'change his socks regularly and keep his bowels open'. He imagined they were composed to remind him of another, much happier, world but whatever their content, her letters were his antidote to solitude and isolation; he read them so often he could recite whole paragraphs to himself while on patrol.

He had tried to play the man by talking to Revell. Or so he had convinced himself. But they had seen little of each other after that evening in Noeux until yesterday, and circumstances dictated their conversation was too trivial to warrant a blurted confession of love for the man's fiancée. Now he had the time to confess it was too late. This was no moment to broach a subject that could distract them from the task in hand. If their minds wandered in the next 12 hours both of them could quite easily wind up dead.

Max stretched and twisted. He shifted his weight from one deadened buttock to the other but still found no rest. Now he curled himself into a ball imagining himself next to Rowan Hawes. Then it was Zena he fantasized, and the memory of responsive flesh. This only made sleep more elusive. He tried to occupy his mind with less erotic thoughts. He imagined himself fishing in The Shallows, casting his line under the banks below the lasher where he knew the wiliest and fattest perch would be hiding. He watched his float bob, struck hard and fast, and waited for the flash of black, silver and gold to break the surface to be hauled into his keep net. Then he listed the five best tries he'd ever scored in his rugby career, reliving the ecstasy of hurling his body through the air and bouncing over the try-line for the winning score. All these memories contrived to do, however, was to leave him wider awake.

Max listened for the sound of snoring coming from Revell's cot; hearing only yawning guessed he must also be awake. Revell was trying harder than he to lie dormant, which made Max's attempts all the more theatrical. He grunted and turned his pillow over to the fresher side, pumped it up and wedged his hands underneath.

'Can't you sleep either, Max?'

'No.'

'Want to talk?'

Max was convinced he could hear his heart thumping despite layers of clothes, blankets and groundsheets. Here was his chance.

'Rather not,' Revell said after some reflection. 'Best try to get some sleep if we possibly can.'

Still no sleep came. It could not vanquish yesterday's news.

The Battalion had marched from Goldfish Chateau to relieve a portion of the front near Wieltje in readiness for an assault on German lines north of St Julien. These lines were protected by numerous concrete pillboxes. Chief among these machine-gun nests was that at Pond Farm. If this pillbox could not be eliminated prior to the main attack it would undoubtedly founder. Adamson informed Max that GHQ had taken the view the most effective method of removing this obstacle was by stealth: a small group getting close in under the cover of darkness and destroying it with bombs. As Revell knew the terrain from previous Ypres campaigns he was given command and told to select a handful of veterans for the job. Adamson said that Revell had no hesitation in requesting Max should be one of them.

Max had sloped back to his dugout debating whether Revell had somehow got to know of his tryst with Rowan Hawes and this was his way of exacting revenge. It would not be difficult for Revell to put him in the way of a bullet on a mission like this one: at night, through no-mans-land, few witnesses. Max was ordered to pick two men to complete the party. He selected Bostock and Dewe. Better the devils he knew, he reasoned.

The quartet assembled at midnight in Capricorn Trench that ran parallel to the St Julien—Passchendaele road, wrapped in a shawl of darkness. They steeled themselves against the cold by wearing woollen vests and cardigans beneath their tunics and an extra pair of thick socks on their feet. They'd blackened their faces with burnt cork, and Bostock and Dewe had dulled their bayonets with a covering sock to counter any glitter in the light of the moon or from a star shell. Revell and Max were armed with revolvers not rifles, but they all carried knives and packs weighed down with the Mills bombs they would use to knock out the pillbox.

Revell drew his revolver and led them in single file along the forward sap toward no-mans-land. An arc of flame from the German shells that routinely passed overhead silhouetted the ruins of Ypres to their rear and cast a shimmering rainbow on the water filling every crater and ditch that lay in front of them. The din from tonight's shells seemed all the louder and threatening for their exposed position.

They halted at the end of the sap and rested their backs against the wicker revetment of the trench awaiting Revell's signal to scramble over the parapet. Max looked across at Bostock and Dewe. They seemed to be in a trance. Their lips curled with dryness; their mouths hung open like bewildered bloodhounds. And their eyes were watering away their camouflage with a salty sharpness he could almost taste. The taste of fear. He knew he must look no different, because he, too, felt as if he was about to pee himself.

None of them had been in such a vulnerable position since the raid on Fayet; as they had that night, they felt death's beckoning finger. The silences between shells seemed to lengthen and only made the subsequent explosion more nerve-shattering. Max told himself to think of it like the gap between lightning and thunder: the bigger the gap the safer you were. That's what he always told himself, but it never had been a theory convincing enough to repel the sensation of imminent diarrhoea. And nor did it now.

Max reached into his pocket and produced a flask of rum. He took a swig and felt the heat trickle down his gullet and through his body until its powers even appeared to have dried out the wetness in his socks. He handed the flask to Revell, who took a quick sip before passing it to Bostock and Dewe—who drained the contents between them. They gripped their weapons and scrambled over the top.

Pond Farm lay dead ahead, 500 yards away across open ground. It began to rain, thick curtains of rain driving into their faces and running down into their boots, forcing them to adopt an unnaturally low crouch. By the light of falling star shells they picked their way around the shell-holes and through the detritus of battle: shattered limbers, some with rotting horses still hanging between the shafts; and scores of stinking human carcasses, both British and German. The length of time they had been lying where they died was evident from their colour: from white to yellow, to yellowish green, to black. That and their size: with each passing day girths and faces expanded to become as taut and globular as balloons. Many bodies lay with their pockets turned out, personal letters and photographs protruding but, invariably, anything of value pilfered.

And the stench. All armies smell when in the field. But the smell of living troops was quite distinct from that of dead ones. It was like visiting the field latrine after someone who'd been gorging himself on hard-boiled eggs and cabbage fried in bacon fat. The stench, vaguely sweet and acutely pungent, made them want to heave and forced them to pull their scarves up over their noses.

They plugged on, sliding and slithering over the freshly greased mud, falling and recovering, desperately trying not to make a sound of fatal volume, until Revell halted and jabbed a finger in the direction of what appeared to be the remnants of a farm gate up ahead to the right. They peered through the sheeting rain.

It seemed to Max as if there was someone leaning against the gate. Revell made a throat-cutting gesture and waved Bostock forward. They pressed themselves down into the mud, listening to it squelch against their cheeks, feeling it glue sodden clothe to cold skin, and watched Bostock worm his way toward the gate, drawn bayonet between his teeth. Max's fists clung to the mud, balling a sausage in each hand, fearing his heart was thumping loud enough to alert any German within 100 yards.

Suddenly Bostock stopped and sat up. His head slumped down onto his chest. Max and Revell swapped shrugs. There had been no crack of a sniper's bullet, no movement from the figure at the gate. Perhaps it was just a freak shadow. They relaxed.

Revell led them up to Bostock, who was struggling to get his breath and snuffling from a combination of rain and tears. Bostock didn't want them to see the pathetic state he was in, and wiping the back of his hand across his face he thought of all the Huns being incinerated inside that pillbox once he'd lobbed his bombs in their laps. His expression hardened, and he pointed toward the gate.

The figure Max thought he'd seen was no sentry. It was the corpse of a dead Tommy, the skin of his face grinning tight, pulled back as if his skull was fighting to get out. In life he had possessed a pair of fine bushy eyebrows and a short, squat nose, but in death they now played a minor role in his appearance. It was his arms that attracted the attention. They were outstretched at right angles to his body and a bayonet had been thrust through each palm into the top bar of the gate.

Max retched, his revulsion and hatred spewing from him in a torrent of vomit. He'd heard tales of Germans crucifying wounded men and leaving them to die, but he had always refused to accept that any enemy could be so despicably evil. For the first time he felt the compulsion to kill, he wanted to see the look on a German's face when the bullet tore into his chest or the knife ripped open his guts. He wanted more than killing: he felt the overwhelming urge to inflict pain.

Then a shriek so high-pitched it was almost inaudible caused Max to jump. He brandished his Webley, expecting Germans to be upon them any second. But the pitiful sound was coming from Dewe. He was wailing. He wriggled over to him and clamped a hand over his mouth. Dewe was quaking like the victim of an exorcism. He had endured one day too many and wanted the torment to end. His head was full of dismembered limbs, of a snivelling boy tied to a chair at Caulaincourt and the broken body of Arthur Goodey lying beneath a shattered tree.

Dewe decided he was going home. Back to the farm. Back to the clear air of an English cornfield. Back to milking his cows and enjoying a pint of Morrells and a game of cribbage in The George of an evening. He fought Max off, screaming like a mad man. Max had never felt more terrified in his life. Not even on the Black Bridge. He braced himself for the bullets.

'Shut him up!' hissed Revell. 'For Christ's sake, Max! Kill him if you have to or we're all dead!'

Max drew his knife. There was nothing else he could do. Revell was right.

Dewe stood up. 'Fuckin' Hun bastards!' he cried. 'I'm going to find the bastard that killed Arthur and strangle 'im with me bare 'ands!'

He threw down his rifle and staggered blindly onward into the rain, singing *It's a Long Way to Tipperary* at the top of his voice, just as a star shell burst overhead.

Max shook: their position was blown; mortars would soon open up. They heard the whistle signalling the first one being prepared, and the three of them turned into crazy men, instinctively digging-in, all thoughts of Dewe erased.

But the notion of digging-in was ridiculous. They couldn't dig through water and merely threw up ridges of useless slush. They heard the woof-woof-woof of the drum, loaded with 200lb of wet yellow paste that smelt heavenly of marzipan but would send them to hell, spinning end over end through the air toward them and waited for its slow demoralizing descent and their destruction. It was too late to pray to God. So they cursed him instead.

The missile whorred into the mud 50 yards in front of them, bursting with a force that sent a shock wave through the muddy soil as if it truly were water, and leaving a crater the size of a living room. Layered with brown filth, they shook where they lay. But none of them tried to move. They dare not since German practice meant there was sure to be another. And they never landed in the same place.

'Stay where you are!' Max yelled—and began counting the seconds.

He reached five. The wait seemed endless. Like those cricket matches when he'd been fielding in the deep, waiting for another skier to be hit his way, anticipating the flight of that rock-hard leather ball, dreading its stinging arrival. He got to ten. His eyes resembled shaking dice. Now he felt as if he was locked in the pillory, exposed and helpless, and begged it would be clods of earth or even bits of corpses about to thud into him rather than white-hot shards of eviscerating metal.

Pheee . . . shtump! A second shell smacked into the mud just yards in front of Dewe.

Max watched a roman candle of flame comprising hundreds of pieces of shrapnel shoot outwards like the petals of a blooming flower. He heard Dewe get as far as saying goodbye to Piccadilly but not as far as bidding farewell to Leicester Square. The singing stopped. He heard the whine. And he saw Dewe decapitated as if with one clean blow from a chopper, his body stumbling on for few more steps in the manner of a slaughtered chicken before pitching forward in a heap.

Max screwed his eyes until they hurt and rolled over onto his back, waiting for death. But all that came was the sound of groaning and someone calling his name. Revell had been hit.

Max crawled across to him. He was breathing with a rattle. The cause was obvious: he'd a jagged hole in his chest. Shrapnel had pierced him below the left shoulder blade and exited under the collar bone, exposing his lung. Max looked down into the grey features of a man who was dying, and knew it. He pulled open Revell's tunic and eased the braces off his shoulder, and then tried to staunch the flow of frothy blood with an emergency field dressing.

'Stay quiet, Peter,' he murmured. 'We'll get you to an aid post.'

Revell asked for water but Max, knowing the consequences of that for a chest wound, refused. Instead he rubbed the rain on Revell's face around his lips.

'Leave me!' Revell moaned.

'No. You'll die out here on your own. I'll get you back. Trust me.'

Max looked around for Bostock. There was no sign of him. He couldn't risk calling out for him. The barrage had ceased, but the Germans were loosing sporadic bursts of machine-gun fire and a patrol might be on its way. He dragged Revell up on his feet, took firm hold of one of his arms and began to walk. Each skidding, lurching step squeezed another groan from him, his blood oozing down his dangling braces to puddle in the folds of his trousers.

Yard by yard and shell-hole by shell-hole they edged back toward the safety of Capricorn Trench, but with each step Revell became heavier and Max felt wearier. He began to wish Revell would die. If he did not, they both would.

A line of bullets pinged into the mud behind them like fireworks, causing them to slide into the nearest shell-hole. They found themselves up to their waists in freezing liquid mud and began shivering uncontrollably. Revell's breathing was coming in short rasps now and the blood from his chest wound cut a meandering course across the slime.

Max looked at Revell. His eyes were shut. He felt his neck for a pulse and put his ear to Revell's chest. He was still alive. His body was shattered but the man was refusing to die. A gurgling and moaning came from his throat, now high and liquid, now low and dry. Max wanted him to die. Needed him to die. And quickly. It would be best for him. And it would be best for himself. On both counts. He could not afford to stay here any longer. He saw her face and he knew unequivocally that he wanted Revell to die. He had to die. If Revell were dead, she would be his.

He looked at his watch: in an hour he estimated they had made no more than 30 yards. That decided him. Folding Revell's arms across his chest, he kissed him on the forehead. Then he clambered out of the crater and started hauling himself through the mud using his shoulders and hips in a serpentine wiggle. He urged himself onward, terrified of losing concentration and slipping into one of the water-filled craters to drown. But he felt no pain, only an extreme tiredness that made him want to curl up into a ball and sleep. Soon he became two men, his mind leaving his body and racing on ahead to watch his other tear-streaked self struggling to keep up.

Max dragged himself upright, no longer caring whether he was hit or not, and forced one foot in front of the other. The knowledge of what he'd just done started to choke him and he began to cry, every drop of humanity seeping out of him at the thought of leaving a comrade to die alone, uncomforted, with no consoling hand to hold.

Then he saw her face once more, like a vision sent to inspire him, come to rescue him. His twin selves were reunited and he became whole. He accepted his guilt and its cause; why he had committed the soldier's unforgivable sin. He wiped the mud and rain from his face and found he was no longer trembling. The way was now clear for him to claim her. He scrambled on, toward her, slowly narrowing the gap between them.

From the next shell-hole someone had observed Max's anguished progress with mounting fascination. Hector Bostock grinned. Then he chuckled. God was a blacksmith. God had preserved Hector Bostock, and he planned to profit from what he had just witnessed. He would make Max Lanham wish he had stayed in that shell hole with his dead officer pal.

17

Hill 35

It took Max another hour to reach safety and report the failure of their mission, by which time the main attack was underway. After holding up the Battalion's advance for much of the day, Pond Farm was taken with considerable losses but withering enemy fire eventually forced the Battalion to withdraw, conceding any ground it had won.

Max heard the news as he slurped from a mug of hot soup poured for him by a surprised mess orderly who told him he had been reported missing, presumed dead, by the sole survivor of his party, Private Bostock.

Max finished the last of the soup and went looking for Bostock. He found him in the Battalion dressing station, sat drinking tea while a bandage was being applied to his right hand by an orderly.

'Where the hell did you get to?' said Max.

Bostock sipped his tea for a moment before answering. 'Thought you wuz dead, sir. So I lay low for a bit, an' then made the best of me way back.'

'Did you not see me and Captain Revell? Could you not have helped?'

'Well, sir, it was rainin' bloomin' hard, an' visibility was lousy . . .'

'Any excuse, eh?' Max growled, leaning over until he could bite Bostock's ear if he so chose. 'Why couldn't it have been you instead of Sam Dewe!'

Bostock picked up his mug and took another mouthful. 'And you might have been the unlucky one instead of Cap'n Revell . . .'

'What do you mean?'

'Well, now you've jogged me memory loik, I might've seen summut.'

Max suddenly felt as cold as he had in the fox-hole.

'He was unlucky, weren't he? The way I saw it, the way I heard it, he had some life left in 'im when you . . .'

'Really?'

'You know, when you folded his arms an' kissed him on the for'ead loik a big Jessie?' said Bostock, pulling a girlie face.

'It's your word against mine,' Max hissed. But his words bore little conviction in his own mind. He knew he'd never been a convincing liar—which was one reason why he tended toward telling the truth.

Bostock glanced furtively left and right, and craned forward to speak in a voice scarcely above a whisper. 'Thass as maybe. But it en't goin' to do you any favours in the mess, issit? Specially when they hear about you an' Captain Revell's fiancée.'

Max chewed his lip, trying to marshal his thoughts.

'Me brother gave me all the gen. Pretty lively it sounds an' all!'

'Are you blackmailing me?'

'What, me?' said Bostock. He folded his arms.

'If you are,' said Max with a laugh, 'you must be begging for every available shit detail?'

'No, Mister Lanham,' said Bostock, straightening his back and fixing Max with pupils like lances. 'I'm 'xpectin' the 'xact opposite. I waunt more than me share of every cushy job goin'. That way I'll be too busy to think about openin' me mouth.'

Max stared at Bostock's bandaged hand, playing for time, trying hard to think of a feasible solution. 'I suppose that's self-inflicted, just in case you need an alternative option?'

Bostock grinned. 'Why not? Tried VD but the MO wasn't wearin' that dodge, wuz he! Thought about shootin' me trigger finger off, but a finger comes in 'andy, if you know what I mean? You've gotter keep tryin' though, haven't you? I mean, I'd be grateful if you could put me on the loaders an' leaders team.'

'I'm sure you would,' Max replied, laughing.

Loading the mule trains and leading them forward during advances was a sure method of escaping all share in the fighting—a perk Max had no intention of gifting a malingerer like Bostock.

'Oh, an' one other thing,' said Bostock, tapping out each word with a finger. 'Stay away from Zena Boas. She's my girl. Keep your 'ands off!'

Max marched out of the tent, angrily chewing an imaginary nut. He had given himself no choice. Bostock would need to be dealt with. And soon.

The following day the clouds hung low and the sky darkened to Hades. When it seemed there could be no more moisture left in the sky it began to rain yet again. For 24 whole hours it rained. It rained for the following 24 hours also. Then for another 24 hours accompanied by thunderstorms matching any bombardment in their frightening intensity. And then for yet another 24 hours. It was an unremitting deluge that sculpted a cratered wilderness of mud along the horizon and reduced virtually every sodden man to coughing and sneezing as he stood-to at dawn. But of more import to Max, this endless downpour ensured a period of relative calm in which every man in the platoon might be allocated a cushy job, not just Bostock. It also gave him time to think.

The stronghold at Pond Farm was eventually reduced by barrage three days after Revell's abortive mission, thus precipitating an attack on the next strongpoint in the German line, the massed gun-pits on Hill 35. Over the course of several nights, patrols were sent out to ensure all abandoned enemy trenches were free of booby-traps, and that all wire was cut ready for the main push on 10 September. Max volunteered to make the last reconnaissance. And he'd decided who he was taking with him.

He found Bostock hidden behind a groundsheet in a sub-parapet cubbyhole. He was fast asleep on one of the standard issue wooden frames driven into the trench wall, in effect little more than a box made of planks on which the men might try to sleep. Tucked up in the foetal position, his knees were doubling as a pillow, his legs pulled back safe from passers-by.

Noting his evident discomfort with a twisted smile, Max shook him roughly by the shoulder until he stirred. Bostock growled and cocked a fist at his intruder until he saw who it was. 'Thought you'd let a man finish his kip, sir!'

His head spun and he cursed Max roundly under his breath. Two hours dozing on a plank, half sinking into a dream-ridden sleep, half hearing every noise within earshot, had yielded scant rest for body or mind. On such a hard bed even his well muscled flesh offered no support. Bone pressed down and the wood pressed up; sandwiched in between was a maze of crossed nerves. His arms were stiff and he'd lost all feeling in his feet, which now seemed to be residing in a different land to the rest of him. He swung his lower body out into the trench and attempted to stand up, but his knees had not regained anything like full strength and he had to steady himself by reaching out for the parapet. Even by Bostock's high standards it was fair to say his mood was foul.

'Bostock, you and I have volunteered for a wire-cutting detail tonight.'

'Like buggery I 'ave!'

'Wouldn't you rather be seen to volunteer for an op tonight and earn the right to be considered for a load-and-lead job when the assault on Hill 35 kicks off? Or would you prefer the options the other way round? I know which I think is the cushier number.' Bostock rubbed his nose, deep in thought. 'Roight, then.'

'Look sharp!' said Max. 'You've got 40 minutes to get your dinner before rendezvousing with me at Pommern Castle.'

Bostock shook and rubbed his limbs back to life while searching for a dixie. If one thing mattered to a soldier more than sleep it was food—run close, perhaps, by letters from home. Which one topped his priorities was dependent upon which one currently occupied his mind. Right now Bostock was hungry and time was not on his side. Trench life, however, had taught him ingenuity. He tore up some canvas sacking and smeared it with candle-grease before pushing it into the bottom of a blackened Maconachie tin. Thrusting his bayonet into the side of the trench, he looped the tin's makeshift wire handle over it, lit his tinder and placed the dixie on top of the improvised stove. In went some beans and bits of bacon. The smell of cooking bacon soon attracted the younger members of 16 platoon but one glance at Bostock's heavy-lidded welcome sent these trench vultures packing. Then he heated a billy of water for a lukewarm mug of tea, rolled a cigarette for afterwards, and sank onto his haunches to eat his supper using the lid of a tobacco tin. Bostock surveyed the shiny tin lid that had served as his plate, licked the tip of his finger and dabbed the surface to ensure he'd consumed every last morsel of bacon rind. He took a long drag on his roll-up and puffed a series of smoke rings across the trench. He could find no fault with Max Lanham's reasoning. And that's what unsettled him.

They met in the front trenches known to the troops as Pommern Castle, and started along the tortuous track of tipsy duckboards that led toward the most advanced corner. The duckboards were now so lopsided from the pounding of countless feet and the bottomless mud beneath that it was increasingly difficult to stand up or make progress on occasions without the two men holding onto each other. The farther they got the grislier the walk became: two dead bearers holding a stretcher carrying a rotting corpse being gorged by rats; a hand, nothing else, clinging to the parapet; a Tommy prostrate on his back with his brain squeezing out of head like paint from a tube. a dead signaller clutching a basket still containing pigeons. Max unclipped the flap, and they watched one bird fly away to freedom; the other was too weak and Bostock dispatched it with a flick of his wrist.

Eventually, after a walk that should have taken five minutes but required fifteen, they reached the apex of the front line. A shaky-voiced sentry told them not to linger as the vicinity had taken a direct mortar hit a short time earlier. Max drew his revolver and peered over the parapet. It was as if he was back on holiday at Brancaster, scanning the mudflats for curlew and peewits: everywhere seemed covered in water, dappled and sparkling in the moonlight like slivers of mercury. Pockets of mist swirled from one lake to another, dropping a blanket of false tranquility over the scene and deadening, though not muffling completely, the various noises of the battlefield—the distant poop-poop of a mortar and the occasional short chattering burst from machine gun—until a man might convince himself it was perfectly safe for him to wander at will.

Max filled his lungs with air and vaulted up and over the parapet, beckoning Bostock to follow. He pointed to a line of wire twinkling in the moonlight and they waddled toward it, picking a careful path between craters and dead bodies. Negotiating the lip of a water-filled shell-hole a sudden explosion of air made Max jump. It was no trout rising to the fly, only a dead Hun, his bloated body filling his uniform as snugly as a glove. Max held his nose. Somehow German dead smelt differently to British, more like rotting cabbage. He reasoned it must be something to do with their rations, all that *sauerkraut*.

They reached the wire and Max mouthed instructions to Bostock, who commenced snipping. Max felt his knees shaking beneath him as he attempted to lock his legs out. When they refused to obey, he wondered whether this was an omen, a sign to abort his plan, scrub all thought of it as if he had never even contemplated it. Then his lips parted. He thought of Bostock mocking a dying Arthur Goodey; making love to Zena. His skin prickled at the memory of the ridicule he was subjected to on the Black Bridge, the scorn he endured before, during and after the ordeal; now Bostock stood between himself and the hope of lasting happiness with the woman he loved. Damn it, Bostock deserves what's coming to him.

Max slowly knelt down behind Bostock and, equally deliberately, raised his Webley until it was an inch from the back of Bostock's head. He convinced himself that everything he wanted in the future rested on him squeezing the trigger. No one would know. Rowan Hawes need never know. Just as she didn't need to know the circumstances of Peter Revell's death. All he need do was square it with his conscience. He squinted down the barrel and pursed his lips. Just one little squeeze was all it needed. One squeeze and he would be free. But his hand began shaking. He couldn't control his hand. His fingers curled like salted slugs.

Bostock felt something brushing against the back of his head, ceased snipping and looked over his shoulder. 'What the fuckin' hell!'

He knocked the revolver sideways. The trigger guard caught on Max's finger and the gun went off, throwing Bostock backwards until he teetered on the lip of the shell-hole. His outstretched arms flailed as he tried to keep his balance, but the mud was too treacherous and he fell backwards, his body punching a hole through the mist-covered slime.

The mud dragged him down up to the neck. His mouth opened and shut like one of Baggy Lones's pike on its way to the net as he found the strength to extricate his right arm and plead for help.

Max told himself it was no use trying to save him. The mud had claimed him. He picked up Bostock's rifle and aimed it between

Bostock's eyes. 'Now you know how Goodey felt when he was about to die!'

Max's finger closed on the trigger. This time his hands were not trembling. They were purposeful.

Then his trigger finger straightened again. His conscience objected. Max swung the rifle round, and held it out for Bostock to grab. Bostock clawed the air frantically until his fingers fastened onto the rifle. Bit by bit he managed to wrap his hand round the stock and Max began to pull.

'Can't do it, eh?' wheezed Bostock. 'Knew you 'ad no fuckin' guts!'

Max watched a tablecloth of mist descend upon Bostock's face, and when it floated away the features that re-emerged had turned into his own. In that moment he saw Bostock for what he was: his nemesis. In Bostock he saw himself. Bostock amounted to a daily reminder of a man he despised, the member of a family he despised. Now he could be rid of that man. Then nothing would lie between him and happiness with Rowan Hawes.

Max's teeth bared like those of a week-old corpse. He stopped pulling and began to push. Out of the mist he saw Arthur Goodey walking towards him, hands outstretched, holding his entrails like Marley's ghost dragging his chains. Alongside him marched a headless yet still singing Sam Dewe carrying the disembodied head of Peter Revell under his arm. They all exhorted him to push harder.

Max locked both hands on the barrel, and shoved with every atom of hate in his body until the rifle butt jammed under Bostock's jawbone, thrusting his head back and beneath the mud. Bostock felt the cloying muck force the last particles of air from his lungs and he felt his fingers twitch thin air. Then they slid beneath the mud.

Max let out a loud grunt at a job well done as he watched the ginger head and flapping hands sucked from view, watching the mud bubble like lava for a few seconds before the ripples dispersed. He stood up, tilted his head back and roared out his emotions like King Lear, months of guilt, years of frustration, a lifetime of bitterness, pouring out of him like an ejaculate. Suddenly he felt the happiest he'd been since that night at the Holywell Music Room: this was one next-of-kin letter he would enjoy writing. He examined his hands. They were rock-steady.

He felt no remorse. He laughed, a schoolboy giggle gradually giving way to a rugby player's guffaw.

That's when he felt a tingling sensation around his nostrils and began spluttering. He peered down into the shell-hole through watering eyes and instantly became aware of the pungent smell of garlic and onions.

He felt for his gas mask. And began counting to six.

18

Boulogne

Captain Max Lanham MC and Rowan Hawes BA were married in Iffley's church of St Mary the Virgin in August 1919 shortly after the bride had completed her part-time studies at St Hugh's College and taken her external degree. They became neighbours of Ben Newsam in Church Way, purchasing Rivermead, and raised three children, two girls and a boy. The girls developed into gifted musicians, attending the Royal Academy, one a violinist the other a soprano. The boy, whom they named Peter, achieved what his father had not by going up to Exeter College as an undergraduate and winning his Blue at rugby. After some initial setbacks, Max built a career for himself as a writer and became a published novelist. Rowan threw her energies into teaching but her penchant for good works saw her drawn increasingly toward local politics: she became the first woman elected to Iffley parish council and later successfully stood as a parliamentary candidate for the Oxford South constituency; she also revived the fortunes of the Iffley Choral Society by staging an *al fresco* production of *The Messiah* in the gardens at Rivermead. Each summer they holidayed for one week on the Suffolk coast in a rented house in Aldeburgh followed by another in the top-floor apartments of the Palazzetta San Lio in Venice, the better to pursue their love of the sea, art and opera. Their troubles were few. Their days were full of laughter and their nights replete with sighs.

Max hallucinated throughout the weeks he drifted in and out of consciousness while lying in the casualty clearing stations to the north-east of Ypres around Proven—known affectionately to the troops as Mendinghem, Bandagehem and Dosinghem. But although he also experienced flashes of Peter Revell and Hector Bostock toiling alongside him in that endless sea of mud, such bleak imagery was soon swamped by fantasies illustrating his future with Rowan Hawes. By the time his fever, and the danger of pneumonia from secondary infection, had passed and he was transferred by rickety ambulance train to the base hospital at Boulogne, he'd blotted out all memory of the disturbing events associated with his final two patrols. They receded along with the sound of gunfire until gone completely.

Max was lucky. He was one of the 250,000 casualties sustained by the Allies during the three months of Third Ypres, but not one of the 100,000 who died. The gas drills at Broxeele had proved his salvation. He lay in a shell-hole for 12 hours before being discovered during a routine search of no-mans-land by regimental stretcher-bearers. They found him delirious, his forehead and forearms dotted with blisters reminiscent of freshly-watered red carnations.

The respirator saved Max's lungs from being incinerated. He was taught to breathe low and shallow for the first month so as not to put pressure on any damaged membranes. Meanwhile, the first-degree burns on his hands and face were coated with oil, the only treatment available apart from shots of morphine to relieve the constant pain, and he was fed a diet of Guinness and milk pudding to protect and flush out his digestive system.

The hospital at Boulogne was a commandeered nunnery on the edge of the old town, on the coast road to Wimereux. From his bed on the ground floor he enjoyed a view of the sea when the doors were tied back on the few days of fine weather; then he might day-dream of the girl waiting for him on the far side of the Channel, medicine beyond any the doctors could prescribe. One of the nurses took a shine to him—a pert-nosed girl from Cambridge with wonky teeth, an infectious smile and sunny disposition—but he seldom returned her interest with anything more sociable than a grunting 'Yes,' 'No' or 'Thank you.'

After a month of bed-rest, he was permitted to leave the ward each afternoon and encouraged to walk out of the hospital compound, even to cross the bridge into the town. He soon struck up an acquaintance with an old woman selling roasted chestnuts at the far end of the bridge. With her leathery olive skin and sickle-bent body, she reminded him of Granny Jake, and he was wont to test his poor French by sitting beside her in front of her charcoal fire, telling her about Rowan Hawes. The old dear would laugh at the mad young Englishman's nonsensical French until sharp veins crackled around her eyes, but he was more than glad to have a captive audience whom he might regale with thoughts he could not share with anyone else even though he sensed she barely understood them. The old dear had one other beneficial effect. She taught him how to laugh again.

There were other, less pleasant, daily reminders of how lucky he had been. The bed next to his in the gas ward contained a 19-year-old private lying beneath a tent of propped-up sheets. The doc, a thin sandy-haired Glaswegian with amused eyes and the soft hands of a poker player, told Max the boy had one collapsed lung and a haemorrhaging stomach; in addition most of his skin had been flayed, his teeth were a rotting yellow and his black hair needed cutting, which accentuated the transparency of what skin he retained. Max tried to offer words of encouragement or conduct a one-sided conversation to cheer him up, but the only sound he heard him utter by way of reply was a wheezing plea to let him die. After two weeks the boy got his wish, providing one of the many funerals Max was able to watch in the course of his two-month stay.

Although the nurses—mostly nuns and society girls of the Voluntary Aid—healed the wounds to Max's body, those to his spirit were more obstinate. They read to him and conversed with him whenever they could find a moment, which was understandably seldom. But the cure for Max's brand of depression was not within their power. The required elixir amounted to letters from home. He received a constant stream from his mother. But none arrived from Rowan Hawes.

Max had never needed any incentive to think. And when he had time in abundance he did little but think; and think himself into a funk. He could think of no rational explanation for the absence of correspondence from Rowan Hawes other than the negative. Was she ill? Had she re-assessed her feelings for him, and found them wanting? Obviously she had been informed of Revell's death officially, and would have received his own account by letter: had she detected some unsettling inconsistencies? Had Revell's death crushed her so much she could not countenance the prospect of loving another? Worst of all: was she ashamed of herself for betraying him?

Every day elicited a different answer. Yet it never occurred to a self-centred man that she might be struggling with a guilt and self-doubt of her own; that separation was denying her reassurance; that she might be reticent because she did not want to increase his burden. None of this crossed Max's mind.

He recovered the use of his hands sufficiently to write home. Still no answer came from Rowan Hawes. He even wrote a letter to the Beenhams and another to Newsam in an effort to unravel the puzzle. Still nothing, and as Christmas approached he grew morose to the point of surliness, bickering with fellow patients and chastising his nurses until he forfeited their affection. He went before the medical board on 15 December and was classified Category D: temporarily unfit for service, but likely to become so within six months. Instead of being consigned to the convalescent camp near Rouen, he requested the board evacuate him home on the grounds his progress would be accelerated. His request was granted. He'd be home for Christmas Eve.

All the wounded being repatriated were clustered together in reserved carriages away from men on leave and, unlike the rest of the train, their accommodation was heated with braziers. Uncomfortably so, in Max's opinion, for the heat necessary to keep others warm generated fumes that troubled his bronchial passages. He was given a copy of the *Daily Mail* to read (which did not paint a picture of the Ypres campaign he especially recognized), some chocolate and the totally unexpected treat of an orange, which he proceeded to peel slowly with his pocket knife, cut into segments and suck out the juice before finally consuming the flesh. He made that single orange last from Folkestone to Victoria.

Len Goodey was at Oxford station to meet his early morning train from Paddington.

'Mornin, Master Max,' he said brightly. 'Did you have a good trip?'

'Channel was a mite choppy,' Max replied in kind. 'But, yes, thank you, Goodey.'

Goodey took Max's valise and placed it in the bucket seat before cranking the Morris Oxford's 8.9 horse-power engine into action and climbing into the driver's seat.

'Oh, sorry, Master Max,' he said. 'Would you loik to drive?'

'No thank you.'

Max fixed his gaze on the tower of St George-in-the-Castle as they pottered up the rise to Queen Street wondering how long both of them could maintain this pretence. They continued over Carfax and down the High Street in silence, and were passing All Souls' College before Max found the courage to speak. 'I'm so sorry, Len . . .'

'Mrs Goodey an' me were so grateful for your lovely letter, an' its sentiments,' Goodey replied, without taking his eyes off the road. 'To know you wuz with him at the end an' he didn't suffer meant an awful lot to the missus . . .'

Goodey had been rehearsing this speech for days, but now his shoulders started to roll and his fingers lift off the steering wheel. Max stretched across and pressed them down with a reassuring squeeze. Goodey took a deep breath, sniffed and shook his head. 'Sorry, sir . . .'

'Len, you've nothing to be sorry about. It's me who should be apologizing. Arthur was one of my men. He was my responsibility. I let him down. I let you down . . . Mrs Goodey down.'

Max swallowed and concentrated on Magdalen College Tower, vainly trying to escape by counting its crenellations. But his brain would not let him. Every yard the Morris pop-popped up the Iffley Road brought Rowan Hawes closer to him. He visualized himself running to the door of Nowell House, pulling the bell chain, counting the seconds along to a pounding heartbeat while waiting for her to open the door and fall into his arms.

'Len,' he said. 'Take us through Iffley village, will you.'

Goodey permitted himself a wry smile which he tried to banish without being detected.

'Right you are, sir!' he replied breezily. But he could not help himself. 'That'll be Nowell House, then, will it?'

Max looked aghast at him.

'Miss Hawes?'

'What do you know of Miss Hawes?'

'Well, she came up to the house, didn't she? Called in at the lodge just a'fore dinner time an' the missus directed her . . .'

'When was this?'

'Oh,' Goodey said, thinking for a few seconds. 'Be 'bout a couple of months back, I'd say. Yes, be early October, I reckon. Newmarket races was on! Diadem won again . . . she's won me some money, that filly!'

'Len!' Max said urgently. 'Are you absolutely positive?'

'Oh, yes! Diadem won . . .'

'No!'

'Miss Hawes?' said a startled Goodey. 'Oh, yes. Positive.'

Max thumped the dashboard. 'Then the whole bloody village knows by now!'

'Fraid so,' confirmed Goodey. 'A'course, nobody knew who she were at the start, but didn't take long for some to find out an start gossipin . . .'

'The Bostocks?'

Goodey nodded. 'They'd just lost Hector an all. An' they'd heard you'd come through the same patrol. Couldn't take it. 'Ad to bite back somehow. Only human nature, I s'pose.'

'And what did they tell her at the house?'

Max waited anxiously while Goodey sucked on his dentures. 'Now that I can't tell you. All I know is she didn't stay long cuz the missus saw her walkin' through the gates, head down, glum-like, while she was dishin' up the dinner.'

Max had no time to debate what might have passed between Rowan Hawes and his parents before the Morris stuttered to a halt outside Nowell House. And nor was he about to learn. It was not Rowan Hawes who answered the bell but the housemaid; she informed him that Miss Hawes had returned home to Biggleswade for Christmas and the New Year.

Max slammed the car door. A terrible fear that his mother had said something scabrous fermented in him until it seared his throat with bile. He ordered Goodey to drive as fast as he could to Lawn Upton, and jumped out of the car before it had scrunched up to the front door.

He found his parents in the drawing room, along with the unwelcome sight of Vanessa Devereux. Their expressions of open-faced joy at seeing him vanished the instant he opened his mouth.

'What did you say to her?' he shouted directly at his mother.

'Max! Calm yourself!' she said. 'Why so vexed? Look, Vanessa's here. She's come especially to see you!'

'Well, she can bloody well bugger off again!'

'Max, how dare you . . .'

Max grabbed Vanessa Devereux by the wrist, practically dragging her to the door and shoving her out of the room. He locked the door and put the key in his pocket. 'Now, we're not leaving this room until I get some answers.'

'Max,' his father said, getting to his feet, 'you've been under immense strain . . .'

'Sit down, father! You may, or may not, know what this is all about but she does!' he barked, pointing at his mother.

'She is the cat's mother!' replied Naomi Lanham imperiously. 'If you cannot keep a civil tongue in your head I've nothing to say to you.'

Max knew she meant it. She could stay as uncrackable as a bank vault when she wanted to.

'Very well, mother,' he said as softly and obsequiously as he could. 'I apologize for my outburst.'

'Do sit down, Max,' said his father. 'How about a drink?'

'I'd rather hear what mother said to Miss Hawes first,' replied Max, waving his father's offer aside and staring at his mother. 'Well, mother?'

Naomi Lanham adjusted her seat and lifted her chin. She felt no compunction to speak anything other than the truth but resolved to sugar-coat it for the benefit of an invalid son.

'Yes, Miss Hawes did come to the house . . .'

'I know that! Don't be so bloody evasive!'

Her mouth twisted into a crimson circle.

'Sorry,' mumbled Max, rolling his eyes. 'Please continue.'

'Miss Hawes came here asking of your situation since she had not heard from you in some weeks,' she said haughtily. 'We told her of your injuries and, naturally she was somewhat distressed.'

'Is that all?'

His mother chose to stare vacantly ahead, milking his frustration.

'Mother, was that all?' Max implored.

She redirected her gaze toward him. 'She asked for your precise whereabouts so that she might write.'

'And . . .'

'I told her that would not be appropriate. I told her certain rumours about she and you had come to my attention that, if true, demanded she had no further contact with you.'

'You said what?'

'I don't believe I need repeat myself,' she retorted, head wobbling.

'Is this true?' said Max, turning on his father.

Roy Lanham gave the impression of a petrified man sitting in a dentist's chair. 'I really can't say, Max. I wasn't there.'

'I made the decision on your behalf,' continued Max's mother. 'It was best for your future. You don't want a scandal hanging round your neck. I trusted you to see sense. I knew my decision was what you would have wanted.'

Max picked up the Wemyss pig from the side table and smashed it into the grate.

'You took it upon *yourself*,' he said banging fist into palm, 'to make a decision on *my* behalf, that was *best* for *me!*'

Naomi Lanham recognized some of her own passion in her son's quivering face, and feared she had lost him forever. Her husband saw it too, and bowed his head in sorrow.

'You hypocrite!' bellowed Max. 'You really are the limit! That's the last time you'll stick your nose into my life!'

He stalked out of the room, coming close to breaking the key in the lock, brushed a blubbering Vanessa Devereux aside and went straight to the garage. He cranked the Morris back to life and began the cold 60-mile drive to Biggleswade, alone but for the demons injecting toxins into his brain.

There was only one person who could rescue him now.

19

Biggleswade

Rowan Hawes dropped her placard stating 'Go Forth and Conquer' and grabbed the horse's reins with one hand and proceeded to cut through the leather using the pair of garden secateurs she had brought along in her coat pocket. The animal whinnied and reared up onto its hind legs, depositing its rider in a heap at her feet.

The policeman tore off his helmet and thumped it into her chest. 'If you've harmed one hair of this horse I'll knock you from here to kingdom come!'

The force of the blow sent her reeling, and she collapsed onto the wet pavement, hair matting her face, a groan on her lips. Her appearance was of no concern to her, but the torn hem of her Burberry raincoat did irritate for this would necessitate a third piece of restoration work which even for an expert with a needle and thread like herself was fast becoming tiresome.

'They should lock the lot of you up in an asylum and throw away the bloody key! You're mad, the lot of you! Bloody she-males!'

Rowan struggled to her feet just as another constable yanked her arm behind her back and ripped the suffragette sash of green, white and violet from her breast: green for hope, white for purity and violet for dignity: GWV standing for 'Give Women Votes

'I shall make a note of your number!' she cried.

'Lady, you can draw a picture if you want. It'll not make an 'apporth of difference to the magistrate!'

'You've no right to treat me this way!'

The amused expression on the constable's face stated otherwise. 'Is that a fact?'

She could not avoid yelping with pain—albeit trying her damnedest not to—once he began levering her toward the black maria parked down the street, its rear doors agape in anticipation of welcoming the first visitor of the evening. He shoved her up the steps and pushed her inside. The stench of stale beer and urine bore witness to the van's usual clientele. Rowan pressed her handkerchief to her face but was unable to prevent an involuntary bout of dry retching: she had long ago learnt not to embark on a suffragette demonstration with a full stomach.

'Accommodation not to your liking?' said the constable, slamming the doors shut.

Rowan responded to the shrieks coming from her colleagues still under attack outside by banging her fists on the walls of the van. She visualized the fists, batons and boots brutalizing unprotected female flesh; arms being twisted and thumbs bent back; bodies being hurled from one policeman to another as if they were sacks of grain; and she felt the sting of their cuts and the throbbing of their bruises. And she began to sing, as much to lift the spirits of her comrades as her own, the suffragette words to the tune of *Auld Lang Syne*:

> *They say we are so ignorant*
> *We don't know right from wrong,*
> *But we can tell them what we want*
> *And what we'll have ere long!*

A series of thumps on the sides of her prison made her jump and stop. She took a deep breath and moved on to the movement's version of *John Brown's Body*:

> *Rise up woman! For the fight is hard and long,*
> *Rise in thousands, singing loud a battle song,*
> *Right is might and in its strength we shall be strong,*
> *And the cause goes marching on!*

She was told to 'Shut up!' Repeated warnings followed, each threatening more dire consequences than the last. Still she sang. But after 20 minutes she leant back exhausted, wincing from the pain in her limbs and chest. 'Dear God!' she cried. 'Please help us!'

Then she heard male voices arguing on the other side of the doors. She pressed an ear against the metal, but could not manage to decipher what they were saying. The doors swung open. And there he was.

'Max! It's you!'

She fell into the arms of a man she thought she'd never see, let alone feel, again and folded her own around his neck. He kissed her forehead and looked down into green whirlpools of stored-up emotion: months of worry, anxiety and love swimming to the surface on a current of tears.

'How did you get him to release me?'

'Told him you were Lord Rosebery's favourite niece!'

She felt his body heat invigorating her, his love transfusing into her, and suddenly she felt vibrant and safe. All her pain ebbed away, all her troubles vanished and she began to weep softly against his warm skin.

'Come on Mrs Pankhurst!' he said, carrying her to the car. 'You firebrands can't be trusted left to your own devices! You're coming back to Oxford with me.'

She was tempted to debate the comparison, but reconsidered and merely laughed. 'But my mother . . .'

'We'll stop by on the way. Get you cleaned up. Pick up your bags.'

Max wrapped her in his greatcoat and made her take a sip from his hip flask.

She tried to demur; he pressed it to her lips. 'How did you find me?' she said between coughs.

'Well, Biggleswade's not a big place, and when I heard there was a suffragette march in progress I'd a sneaky feeling where you'd be!'

She laughed again. This time a loud belly laugh. And he joined in. They kissed. She dropped her head onto his shoulder and smelt the sandalwood *eau de cologne* that her senses had tried vainly to recreate throughout the last five months. She snuggled her nose under his ear and inhaled deeply. She soon fell asleep, her dreams populated by Guinevere, Arthur and Lancelot: but this time the romance had a happy ending.

They had reached the outskirts of Aylesbury when the radiator began to protest at the hard work demanded of it since early morning: bubbling and then boiling over with a jet of rusty-coloured steam. Max stopped for petrol and, distracted by his wakening passenger, managed to burn his hand on the hot radiator cap while topping up the water. She stuck the hand under the cold water tap, kissed it better and then wrapped her handkerchief around it before allowing him to continue.

'Max, I've been so worried about you,' she said, 'even more so after Peter's death. The thought of you being killed . . .'

He tried to stop her with a kiss.

'I'd lie awake at night thinking of you, somewhere out there in France, waiting to kill or be killed, and it drove me half-mad!'

He kissed her again.

'How on earth do you cope?' she asked, returning his kiss. 'Just thinking about it sent me into a whirl so what must run through your mind . . .'

'Did you never ask Peter?'

'I did, but he'd never say anything. He'd just make a joke of it and laugh.'

Max exhaled, ready to unburden himself. 'If you really want to know, I'll tell you . . .'

'I do,' she said urgently. 'I do so want to understand.'

'One goes through a jumble of emotions. Beforehand, before you get any sight or sound of the enemy, there's a churning feel of fear and nervousness. Some men vomit—or worse!'

'No!'

'You visualize yourself killing Hun after Hun. But then, when you get within sight of the enemy, you're gripped by a strange hesitancy, you suddenly realize that if you pull the trigger it's highly possible that you're going to kill someone, and it's against human nature to do that. That thought runs round and round your brain until it spins like a carousel at St Giles' Fair and leaves you unable to function. Your finger hovers over the trigger, you wonder whether you can go through with the act of killing another human being and the longer you think about it the more your conscience tells you this is not right.'

Max paused, remembering Bostock and the night when his mind surrendered to the killing instinct.

'But hesitancy can prove fatal. So you have to forget human decency. It's shoot or be shot. Fritz is probably thinking just the same thoughts about you! Of course, if he has fired first it's a different situation. There's no time for thinking. You don't look for any justification, you simply react. Some bastard is shooting at you, so it becomes perfectly acceptable to shoot back! And the more threatened you feel the faster the reaction. The more self-preservation kicks in, the more instinctively you retaliate.'

Max's voice trailed off into the night along with the regular gallery of ghoulish faces parading before his eyes.

She thought she saw tears welling. 'Stop now. I'm sorry I asked.'

'No, it's all right,' Max said, reconsidering her initial question.

She kissed him.

'Do you know the Black Bridge?' he asked.

'Yes, I think so,' she replied, her nose scrunching with puzzlement. 'Isn't that the railway bridge over the Thames just before Iffley Halt?'

'Well,' continued Max, 'waiting to go "over the top" is pretty much like waiting to jump off that bridge!'

'Jump off it? Into the river?'

'Yes!' he laughed.

'How extraordinary! What makes you think that?'

'Because I've been up there waiting to jump!'

'You can't be serious! Why would any sane person want to do that?'

'Precisely my sentiment,' said Max. 'But they do! You see, it's a local boys thing, a sort of rite of passage. All Littlemore boys, when they become teenagers, are challenged to jump off the bridge as a sign of courage . . . reaching manhood. If you don't jump you're no man . . .'

'So, you jumped!'

'Yes, but I didn't want to.'

'Oh,' she said in a voice heavy with disappointment and surprise.

'The whole rigmarole made no sense to me. They dragged me up there, all the village lads, and I stood there thinking about it for a minute or so. It was just a stupid ritual. A convention. You had to do it because you had to do it. That made no sense to me. I got enough of that authoritarian clap-trap from my mother!'

Max gripped the steering wheel tightly with both hands and shook it violently before easing back into his seat.

'So why didn't you just climb down?'

'At the time I gave myself all manner of rational reasons for not jumping,' he said weakly. 'The water's filthy from the oil and the ashes of the trains . . . there's rusty old axles from carts and bits of broken plough you could cut yourself to ribbons on . . . you could break your neck on the plinths that support the pillars under the water . . .'

'Yes, I see . . .'

'But you don't!' Max said, voice rising again. 'None of that was remotely true. I was just plain scared . . .'

'But . . . but you jumped,' she stammered. 'That took courage!'

She looked across at the down-turned mouth and washed-out eyes of a man she had not encountered before.

'You don't understand,' Max mumbled. 'It was the most cowardly thing I've ever done in my life. Scrambling out onto that parapet was the scariest feeling of my entire life, but I was even more scared of climbing down and having to admit to Bostock, Dewe and all the rest that I was too chicken-livered to jump. And so I jumped. Had I been brave I would have come down and looked them all in the eye and told them it was all a meaningless charade, just like I've told you. But I hadn't the guts.'

She watched him choking back the tears and wondered which of these two men she had fallen in love with.

'The memory of that day on the Black Bridge never leaves me. It haunts me. Every time I have to give an order. Every time I have to obey an order. Whether to take the easy way out. Or take the hard way, the right way. Do things I abhor. Things I fear.'

With a contrived cough Max put a final full stop to his confession. He suspected he had said more than enough. Her silence unnerved him; the lack of solace was proving disconcerting. There was much more he was tempted to discuss with her as they drove on through Thame and the Miltons toward Oxford—about Revell, about their future—but he decided to restrict himself to the principal topic stoking a growing headache.

'Rowan,' he said, at length, 'why did you visit Lawn Upton?'

She clasped her hands together as if in prayer. 'When your letters stopped I knew you must have become a casualty. It felt like Peter all over again. I could not eat or sleep. Even the Beenhams noticed. I could hardly function for worrying.'

Max stroked her cheek. 'You cared about me that much? You never said . . .'

'Max, silly Max,' she said. 'If I'd loved you less I could've risked saying more.'

They kissed, and poured out their love for each other between further kisses. Her speech became increasingly rapid, rising and falling on the gulps of air carrying each phrase.

'I went to the barracks but they refused to tell me anything because I was not a next-of-kin, and said I'd have to wait for details to be published in the newspapers. It seemed like an age before I found your name in the list of wounded, but it gave no details of your injuries or whereabouts. So I felt I had no option but to visit Lawn Upton.'

She nibbled her bottom lip and, leaking tears, fixed her gaze on the brightest star.

Max waited patiently for her to continue. But she seemed reluctant to say more. He gently took hold of her chin and turned her head toward him. 'And what exactly did my mother say to you?'

She took two deep breaths. 'She asked me the nature of my business and why I had invited myself to her home. She asked about my employment and my background . . .'

'And?'

'When I told her, she stated that no daughter of a provincial grocer was good enough for her son and that I was not welcome in her home.'

Max thought for a moment, though he really had no need after months of thinking about nothing else, and stopped the car.

'We'll see about that!' he said, holding her two hands in his. 'Rowan, will you marry me?'

20

Iffley Again

Rowan's eyes glistened behind a veil of tears. For the most part they were tears of joy because she had imagined herself, and longed to be, in this situation. But they were also tears of regret because she knew she was not ready to commit herself to any man so soon after Revell's death. It would not be right. And she suspected her candour might wound.

'Oh, Max,' she whispered after an ominously long silence that caused Max to tremble. 'Please give me time.'

Max slumped back in his seat, as if the razors of unrequited love had sliced his bravado to shreds. He exhaled a wisp of disappointed breath into the chill night air and relaxed his grip on her hands.

'I'm not saying "No" to you,' she blurted. 'I just need to get things straight. Peter's death . . . worrying about you . . . your mother's reaction to me . . . and now your sudden return. It's all been too much for me to absorb.'

She reached for his cheek. 'Ask me again in a week or two.'

Max could find no words to do justice to the emptiness he felt inside him, and was on the verge of disgracing himself with tears of his own. He had convinced himself she loved him for what he was, not who he was—a conviction he had never held about Zena. And yet he felt her love ebbing away.

'Max, please promise me you'll ask me again,' she implored. 'Please!'

189

He forced himself to nod his head, and then put the car in gear and drove off. The remainder of the journey passed in an atmosphere befitting such a raw night, both of them keeping their thoughts to themselves. He feeling stupid at giving rein to a presumption that begged self-destruction; she feeling guilty for worshipping an honesty that wounds more than it heals.

He delivered her safely to Nowell House, carried her bags to the door and watched her surprise arrival greeted warmly by the Beenhams. He shouted out 'Merry Christmas!' as the door was closing and she shouted back, asking him to call in the morning.

Max decided to put up for the night at the Tree Hotel rather than face returning to Lawn Upton and the inevitable recriminations. He ate a bowl of stew and dumplings in the bar, but declined an invitation from a party of carol-singers to join their revels around the village once he caught a whiff of the hot rum-toddies they were downing against the cold: it brought the sickly smell of fear back to his nostrils and the clamminess of cold sweat to the creases of his forehead.

He went straight up to his room, bathed and climbed into bed, longing for sleep after two days of almost incessant travelling. It came, albeit cruelly and quickly curtailed. He woke feeling like a damp cabbage leaf. The clack-clacking on the landing sounded like the tramp of boots on duckboards and their message to stay awake if you wished to stay alive. The more he fought for sleep the more elusive it became: one minute he'd be steaming with sweat; the next so cold it hurt to breath. Finally he forsook the prison of the sheets to pace the room. But all he found was Rowan Hawes reclining in each chair or peeping through each window, haunting him with her emerald-eyed smile, her impish wit and her feisty spirit.

Barely 400 yards away Rowan Hawes lay sobbing. Her privations at the hands of the police ensured she drifted into sleep as soon as she felt the blankets caress her neck but she awoke with a start just before three and could never settle again. The crackling silence of a winter's night proved no comforter; just the opposite. She turned her pillow repeatedly and rearranged the sheets to no avail. She could not erase the thought of him having to spend another lonely night in a strange bed and felt the anguish of his loneliness; of him struggling to find inner peace as the very festival of peace dawned; and failing. She wished that bed was hers so that she might soothe his pain with her love. Yet all she could do was press her face into the pillow and cry.

Max greeted Christmas Day from an armchair with less than Scrooge-like jollity. He rubbed the jigsaw of frost from the window pane and peered out at the crystal kingdom beyond. A robin sat on the sill, its feathers fluffed out in search of warmth, its beak pleading for tit-bits. He heard the iron-shod clatter of a passing horse, the milkman's he presumed. The night had been so cold he was obliged to break a thin layer of ice that had formed in his water bowl with his razor before he could shave using kit borrowed from the porter.

Max studied the face staring back at him. It reminded him of the Hun officer he had captured on the Fayet raid: alive and breathing but dead behind the eyes. It was the face of a defeated man. He fingered the small elliptical gold medal hanging from a chain around his neck and, as he had every day in the hospital at Boulogne, read the inscription on the reverse: 'Pray For Us.' He had bought it while on a weekend pass to Paris from a shop peddling religious paraphernalia next to Notre Dame. It was a St Jude medal. He had not one religious bone in his body. But St Jude was the patron saint of lost souls and hopeless causes. He felt that apt at the time and now even more so.

He brushed out his uniform that had hung overnight on the wardrobe door and raided the contents of the porter's shoe-shine box to polish his boots and Sam Browne. Then he dressed and, not feeling remotely like breakfasting or exchanging pleasantries with staff or guests, he decided to walk down to the lock before visiting Nowell House.

The ground was covered with a thin sleet that had frozen, making it and all the bare trees appear as if they had been treated with a coat of icy varnish. The morning air was crisp and clean apart from the faint, but distinct, smell of burning wood drifting from the chimneys, which Max found both evocative and invigorating. Fine Christmassy weather, he thought, as he crunched fresh footsteps across the glassy hotel yard beneath the ancient elm that had been planted in 1614 and gave the establishment its name. A whistling in the topmost branches caused him to look up. He stopped and listened.

The noise grew into the shrill peep of an officer's whistle signalling 'Over the Top!' He began to shake. First his chin. Then his arms. Finally his hips. The swaying branches began to fill with maimed and dying soldiers, calling, shouting, screaming. There were the boyish features of Arthur Goodey asking plaintively whether he was going to die; ashen-skinned Peter Revell begging to be left alone to die in his own arms; a bright-eyed Hector Bostock believing he was going to live. All the memories Max had buried along with the corpses climbed out of their graves in the few seconds he stood transfixed beneath the elm tree. He leant against the trunk and buried his head in the crook of his arm.

His guilt lay heavily on his soul as he waited for the door of Nowell House to open. It demanded retribution. It begged punishment. He feared both. But he was the only source of either.

Rowan greeted him with a full smile and invited him into the sitting room, assuring him they would not be disturbed. His impersonation of a boy who had lost sixpence and found a penny failed to register with her because she had been waiting hours to implement her own agenda. She had made up her mind. He only had to ask her again. She longed to hear him say those four words again and this would be the happiest Christmas of her life.

He sat her down on the sofa and took a seat opposite. She started to speak, but he held up his hands. He began to speak and his words poured forth unchecked, interspersed only with a shake of the head, a thump to the forehead or a bout of nervous marching around the hearth rug that likened him to a caged bear.

His words did not include those she had hoped for. At first she listened to him Expressionless. Gradually she began twisting her handkerchief around her little finger until it whitened, her once happy features fighting a quivering battle with each other none seemed capable of winning.

'So, you see, I took the easy way out and abandoned him. I killed Peter. I left him there to die alone. I was responsible.'

She sat like a block of marble, too cold and opaque to weep; her mouth too acrid for words to form.

'Can you forgive me?' Max asked, bowing his head.

'I don't know,' she replied, haltingly.

She cleared her brain. He was asking her for absolution; asking her to share his guilt, to relieve him of his burden. And her conscience balked. She bit her lip and hid her eyes. She could not, would not, tell a lie, even in circumstances that might have forgiven one.

'Do you love me?' Max asked.

'I don't know,' she answered firmly.

Max yearned for three words, but not these three. He yearned to run his fingers through her hair, stroke the nape of her neck, plant a tender kiss on her mouth, anything to tempt those words from her lips. But he could not. Instead he watched her eyes moisten with a mist he did nothing to disperse. Whether her tears owed most to compassion or love he could not decide. Please God, he prayed, let it not be pity.

He looked into her eyes, no longer crystal clear and inviting. Now they were muddied with sorrow, and he knew instantly the game was up, the ormolu clock on the mantelpiece slowly chiming its way to ten as if tolling the demise of their relationship. His dreams lay before him as tattered as a jester's motley. He felt the devastation drain the strength from his legs, and he leant against the arm of the sofa.

'I'm sorry, Max, so sorry,' she managed to say at last. 'I do care for you, I really and truly do! But everything seems to be crowding in on me. Yesterday. Now this, today. I just can't think straight.'

His obvious distress spurred her compassionate self toward taking that final tentative step, to tell him what he wanted to hear. But another, cooler part of her being, counselled otherwise. That one step involved numerous complications, countless repercussions. Too many people could be hurt by her taking that hazardous step. He would appreciate that.

'I feel I must get away. Be on my own, to think. Get away from here.'

'And get away from me?'

'In a way, yes,' she sobbed. 'Do I grieve Peter's death or rejoice in your love? One rules out the other. I just can't . . .'

She broke off to dry her eyes. 'I thought your love, our love, would overcome anything. Yet what you've just told me makes me think it might not.'

'I understand,' said Max quietly.

'I can't, and don't, blame you for Peter's death. Do believe that.'

He didn't. Why should he. The blame rested with him. He had got what he deserved. Justice had been done. He had bared his soul only for her to punch a hole in it. She had trod on his dreams.

Max walked out into the snow, his eyes shrivelling to 'piss-holes', and felt the heat of tears sting his cheeks. He had not permitted himself to cry since the day his mother spied on him in the bathroom. Not in the yard at Caulaincourt. Not on that wooded ridge above Noeux. And not in the mudbath before Pond Farm.

Now he could not stop himself.

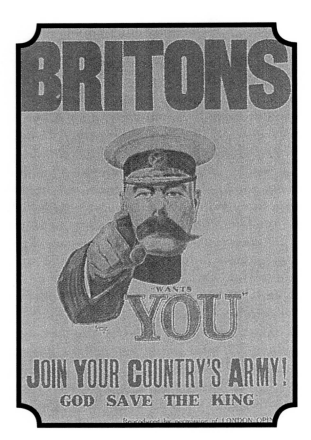

21

Lawn Upton: Part Three

Max hurtled out of Iffley village and hit the brakes of the Morris hard as he met the main road, causing the rear end of the car to skid round and leave it broadside. The right turn took him up Rose Hill to Littlemore. Bearing left led to Cowley. He took only a moment to make up his mind, and swung the car to the left.

In 15 minutes he was drawing up outside the tiny red and orange-bricked Victorian house known as 1, Brasenose Cottages. His Grandpa Jake had worked all his life on Brasenose Farm at the end of the lane, and his widow was granted free occupation of their two-up two-down cottage as a result. He could recall little of Grandpa Jake other than his rotundity, a stubby salt 'n pepper moustache with which he would tickle his infant grandson's cheeks, and his fondness for snuff which he invariably stuck under the little boy's nose just to see him convulse with a fit of sneezing.

Max walked round the house to the back garden where he had enjoyed countless summer afternoons as a toddler, chasing the chickens or staring through the picket fence at the pigs and goats belonging to the Clarkes who lived at number two, or else just splashing about in his grandparents' old tin bath. He halted on the spot where it used to sit and saw his young self giggling naturally and happily, feeling the joy of cool water on a hot day.

A clatter from the scullery drew him to the window and he spied the tiny stooped figure of his grandmother. He paused to look at her closely. The white hedgerow of hair was a mite wilder and her skin slightly yellower thanks to more years of snuff-taking, but apart from that she looked the same as he remembered from his childhood when perched on her knee he'd watched open-mouthed as she dunked toast in her tea. Carefully unlatching the back door, he tiptoed inside, crept up behind her and placed his hands on her hips, causing her to squawk like the chicken she was holding might once have done.

'Gawd!' she warbled, stretching out an arm to find her chair. 'Don't you be doin' that! You silly young bugger! I nearly shit meself!'

Max surprised himself by laughing uproariously at the old lady's salty language, the more so because it was delivered in an Oxfordshire burr so rapid it was almost indecipherable. He had forgotten just how much of a farm girl she had been all her life and her earthiness served as a welcome antidote to her daughter's prissiness.

'Where you bin all these years? Grown a bit since I last seen you. Must be donkeys years!'

She looked him up and down. 'You a sol-jer then?'

'Afraid so Granny,' Max replied, grateful for his uniform diverting attention from his lengthy absence. 'I've another surprise for you! You're coming to Lawn Upton for your Christmas dinner.'

'But I'm just puttin' one of Ethel's bantams in the oven!' she said, waving the spoon she'd just used to baste the bird.

'Well, it'll do for Boxing Day then!' said Max, taking the spoon from her. 'Ditch that pinny and put on your best glad rags and we'll be off! The car's outside.'

Licking her fingers, she smoothed her white carpet of hair and waddled, much like a duck thanks to a bent spine born of years carrying hay bundles and potato sacks from field to cart, over to the kitchen door to lift a grey coat from its hook.

'Don't have much use for this'un any more. But I en't puttin' on any airs 'n graces for her benefit,' she growled.

Granny Jake's shock at seeing her grandson walk into her scullery was low key compared to her daughter's reaction when Max ushered the old lady into Lawn Upton's drawing room. The sight of his mother sinking into a chair, hand to mouth, and the smidgeon of Christmas cheer it brought to his heart, showed itself in the shallow smile that began to scratch his face.

'What's she doing here!'

'Thought you'd like a proper family Christmas at last! Granny Jake's been looking forward to one for years, haven't you Granny?'

The old lady smiled as Max supported her by the elbow while she lowered herself into an unfamiliar chair.

'How about a sherry, Granny?'

Her eyes lit up. 'Thank-you, me boy.'

'What about you mother? Sherry? Or maybe something a trifle stronger in the circumstances?'

His mother shook her head so violently Max fantasized it falling from her shoulders. He was too preoccupied imagining himself hoofing it across the room to guesswhy she could not risk having her thought processes impaired by alcohol.

'Father, a G and T? B and S perhaps?'

Uncharacteristically for Roy Lanham he had made no move to greet a visiting lady and remained rooted in his chair, puffing on a cigarette. He had not seen his mother-in-law for sixteen years, and being reminded of that last encounter made him doubt his legs would support him if he stood. He stubbed out his cigarette. Immediately lighting another, he accepted the generous measure of brandy-and-soda from his son and took a long steady draught.

Max poured an equally large one for himself. 'Well, isn't this pleasant? Cheers everybody. Happy Christmas!'

The logs crackling in the grate matched the atmosphere as the door opened and Rufey entered. 'Ma'am, Mrs Collicutt's here. Asking if she might see Master Max.'

'What? On Christmas Day? She comes here uninvited on Christmas Day! Tell her 'Tell her to come in!' interjected Max. 'It must be important.'

The colour drained from Roy Lanham's face as quickly as the liquid in his glass; he walked over to the drinks cabinet to fortify himself with another.

'Merry Christ . . .' Max got as far as saying when Flo Collicutt entered, before she began babbling as if she were an escapee from the asylum.

'Merry Christmas, Mrs Collicutt,' he said, starting all over again. 'Calm yourself. Have a seat. Will you take a Christmas drink with us?'

He sat her down but she could not keep still. 'It's my Charlie!'

'I see!' said Max knowingly. 'What scrape has Chick got himself into this time?'

Her eyes gushed tears as they flicked from Max to his father and back again. 'He's only gaun an' joined the Army en't he.'

Max rocked with laughter. 'He can't! He's too young!'

'But he has, I tell you! I got a Christmas card yest'dee from my brother, Percy, the one who lives in Reading. Chick was meant to be stayin' with him. He got ever so mis'rable when he heard about your trouble, an' said he waunted to get away for a bit. So I sent him to Percy, they always got on, you see. But Percy's card said he hoped Chick wuz home an' feelin' more chipper. Then t'day I got this postcard. Iss from France!'

She held out the card for Max's inspection.

'What am I goin' to do? What'll I do if they send him to the trenches?'

'Did you know about this mother?'

'No, why on earth should I?'

'You know everything . . .'

'I don't concern myself with the affairs of village boys like Collicutt!'

Roy Lanham's strode past to refill his glass, ignoring both Flo Collicutt's efforts to attract his attention and the glare of his wife, who was fidgeting with discomfort at each sentence Flo Collicutt uttered.

'No need to worry on that score, Mrs Collicutt,' Max reassured her solemnly. 'He's too young to be sent to the Front. If he has managed to join a unit, he'll be restricted to service well in the rear.'

'Can you find him for me?'

'I can't promise anything but I'll see what I can find out.'

Naomi Lanham rang the bell. 'Rufey, Mrs Collicutt is leaving. Will you show her out.'

Flo Collicutt got half-way to the door before she broke down completely. 'Oh, Roy! What are we goin' to do? He's only a baby. You must do summut!'

Roy Lanham responded by taking a large swig from his glass. He glanced at his wife, whose face was a definition of loathing, eyes narrowed and still, mouth thin and straight. He knew, as did she, that they were staring into an abyss which might consume them at any moment. He lit another Gold Flake.

'But Mrs Collicutt,' said Max, 'why should Mr Lanham go to such lengths on Chick's behalf? Chick's not his responsibility.'

'En't he?' said Granny Jake.

'Be quiet, mother!' barked Naomi Lanham.

'No, let her speak,' said a bemused looking Max. Although his grandmother was not blessed with any great range of vocabulary, he knew her choice of words to be nothing less than truthful. 'Go on Granny. What do you mean?'

Granny Jake took a sip of her sherry, paused, and then slowly swilled another around her mouth before swallowing. She had endured a lengthy exile and was not about to let this moment pass any quicker than was necessary. There was little excitement in her life any more. Death was all she had to look forward to these days. Stirring up a spot of mischief was an old woman's prerogative. Especially if it embarrassed her daughter. Her mouth wrapped itself around the lip of her glass and slurped what remained of the sherry.

'The Collicutt boy's his son, en't he,' she said, gesturing toward Roy Lanham.

The accusation penetrated Max like a piece of shrapnel. At least that's what it felt like to him as he fought to reconcile this bizarre accusation, this nonsense, with reality. But one look at his parents was enough to confirm the truth.

Roy Lanham was slumped in his chair, head back, shoulders heaving, hands gripping the arms, tears flowing; Naomi Lanham stood staring into space, all colour siphoned from her immaculately made-up face so that she resembled a geisha.

'Chick Collicutt is my brother? My half-brother?' Max asked, switching his gaze from one occupant of the room to another.

Flo Collicutt nodded. Granny Jake smiled. His parents made no response to their sixteen years of deceit being exposed.

'Y'may as well tell 'im the rest!' chuckled Granny Jake.

'The rest? What rest?'

Naomi Lanham wrung her hands until the knuckles hurt.

'Bout the baby!' said Granny Jake. A'ter he admitted he'd fathered the Collicutt boy, your mother found out she wuz expectin' an' she got rid! Out o' spite!'

'My mother aborted a child! She aborted my brother or sister? Just to spite my father?'

'Max!' cried his mother, reaching out for him. 'She's insane. Why would your father consort with a woman like this!'

'Corse you cut out his co-co! He 'ad to get it somewhere. Only nat'ral!'

'She's rambling. She's old and lost her mind!'

'Have I now? I knows what went on. Next door it were, at number two. Ethel done it. So I knows a'right. Ethel Clarke's bin helpin' out girls in trouble for years!'

Granny Jake pointed at her daughter. 'She knew that well enough. She'd bin to her a'fore, y'see!'

'What?' cried Max.

The old woman slapped her knees and laughed out loud.

'Thought you wuz meant t'be clever?

'Be quiet, mother!'

Granny Jake waved a finger toward her grandson. 'How d'ya think a farm girl like her nabbed a rich feller loik your dad? She'd set 'er cap at him, 'adn't she! So when one o' those fancy artist chums of hers . . . him what gave her that 'oitee-toitee name, her proper name's Nora . . . got her in the fam-lee way, she told that silly bugger over there it were his, and he believed her.'

Max looked at his father and saw the truth in his slumped shoulders and hangdog expression.

'A'corse, your grampy Lanham was no mug,' continued granny Jake. 'He knew his son weren't the sharpest chisel in the drawer, and made her see his quack t' make sure. Once he said she wuz up the duff an' they wuz gunner get married, she got rid o' it, didn't she?'

Max shook his head at what he had just heard and replayed it over again in his mind to make sure.

'She always said she'd get on one way or t'other!'

Granny Jake beamed a smile as big as an open letter box, and held her empty schooner out for replenishment.

'I always knew you were a cold fish,' Max spat at his mother. 'But Medusa herself would have struggled to compete with scheming like this!'

His mother was too intelligent to defend the indefensible any further. She was already contemplating how she could placate her son. Some avenue of escape would present itself if she could just stay in control. A queen is untouchable, she assured herself. They never pay for anything. Not even their mistakes.

'Father, you knew all this?' said Max. 'And did nothing?'

His father rolled the dog-end of his cigarette around his mouth, and clenched the two arms of his chair for the strength to confess his failings to a son he loved but to whom he could show no love. His eyes turned to the portraits of his parents hanging on the wall and flicked from one to the other for some seconds before he was able to manufacture one word: 'Shame.'

'Is that all you can say by way of an explanation?' railed Max.

Roy Lanham extracted a fresh cigarette from the packet, and sat up straight like the officer he'd always yearned to be. He put a match to it with a shaking hand and drew hard.

'Your mother said she'd tell everything, make a right stink, if I left her or acknowledged Chick as mine.'

'So you number blackmail in your list of black arts, do you!' Max shouted at his mother. 'And, I warn you, don't dare contradict or interrupt me!'

At this moment Max did not know whether it was his mother or his father whom he hated more. Rage was eating away at him with the speed of onrushing locusts. Feeling himself losing any vestige of verbal and physical self-control he still retained, he turned back to his father and dropped his voice to a whisper.

'And you believed her? You believed she'd tell the world, her precious society pals, the councillors, the lawyers and the doctors, that she, the imperious my-shit-doesn't—stink Naomi—or should we call her Nora—Lanham, had had two abortions.'

'I . . . I felt under pressure . . .'

'Under pressure!' Max thundered. 'What about the pressure you put on Mrs Collicutt?'

His father was convulsed by a fit of coughing, which ended with him spitting phlegm into his handkerchief and reaching for his B & S.

'I gave her the money for the pub . . .'

'Very magnanimous of you! And what about Chick? Poor sod's grown up never knowing his father lived next door! At least I had this poor excuse for a father! He was denied even that!'

'I took him fishing when I could . . .'

'Well, that makes everything all right then!'

Roy Lanham's eyes hung from his head like dull chandeliers. He sensed his legitimate son standing in front of him and looked up.

'Father,' Max said quietly and controlled. 'You're the biggest fool and most gutless creature I've ever had the misfortune to meet. And you call yourself my father. Chick's the lucky one not me.'

Flo Collicutt ran from the room. Roy Lanham put down his glass and followed her. He paused at the door, gave his wife the withering stare of a condemned prisoner leaving the dock, and then disappeared.

'Roy!' shouted his wife. 'Come back here!'

They heard the front door creak open and then crash shut.

22

Lawn Upton: Part Four

Max drove Granny Jake straight back to Brasenose Cottage. The old woman griped continually about missing her Christmas dinner, but Max paid no heed. She had gone hungry before; she would cope. She was a survivor. He helped her inside and left immediately. He knew he would never see her again.

Nor did he intend seeing his mother after today. He made that abundantly clear to her as soon as Flo Collicutt and his father had fled from the drawing room, and he could not envisage any circumstances that might cause him to change his mind. She was dead to him now; as dead as his unborn sibling. He would return to Lawn Upton to collect his clothes and a few books and be gone from her life forever. As for his father, everything about him was repellent; the sight of his pathetic bankrupt features; the sound of his whining apologetic voice; the smell of his tobacco and alcohol-tainted breath. The very thought of him made Max want to throw up.

He headed back to Iffley. The curtain twitched as the motor died outside Nowell House and Mrs Beenham was at the door before he had time to pull the bell-chain. She informed him Miss Hawes had left the house shortly after he had called; she had asked Mr Beenham if he would drive her to Liverpool where she intended booking passage to Montreal. Had Nowell House collapsed on top of him Max would not have felt one brick.

'Did she leave any word for me?' he mumbled, not knowing where to look.

Mrs Beenham cleared her throat. She was unsure of her reasons other than a profound regard for Peter Revell, but the envelope clutched behind her back stayed where it was despite express instructions to hand it to Max Lanham if ever he should call.

Had Max been allowed to open Rowan's letter he would have read how guilty she had felt at 'betraying' Revell while he was away risking his life, a guilt that weighed even more heavily after his death. She did not blame Max for his death but to run straight into his welcoming arms would amount to loving him on the rebound as opposed to a genuine love. Wondering whether Max would detect these misgivings and come to doubt the honesty of her affections also troubled her. She excused herself by explaining how she needed time to come to terms with her conscience and that this was best tackled alone. She had no wish to hurt Max, although she conceded her flight would undeniably have that effect, and this would haunt her forever. If Max could forgive her and was prepared to wait for her, she prayed there might still be an opportunity for them to be reunited.

Mrs Beenham looked Max squarely in the face and told him Miss Hawes did not wish to be pursued and that she would write in due course once settled in Canada. Then she wished Max 'Good Day' and closed the door. Once back in her drawing room, she shook out a deep breath and threw the letter on the fire.

Max sat in the car, clutching the steering wheel. If he set off now he might easily overhaul them on the road. But would it be the road to Southampton or the road to Liverpool? His heart compelled him to chase after her but his head ordered him otherwise. If he had learnt anything about Rowan Hawes it was that stubbornness ran through her character like a steel girder. She was unlikely to view his disobedience kindly. Or perhaps such an unfettered display of love might do the opposite and win her over?

Max banged his head into his fists. There was no ready-made, sure-fire solution. If he did go after her, eventually the Redcaps would be on his trail. See out the war as unfit for active service and then follow her to Canada might be a better option. By then she might've forgiven him. If she truly loved him as much as he loved her, she would surely come round in time.

He got out of the car and walked up the road to see Ben Newsam. He would advise him the best course of action. He got half-way up the path to Newsam's front door before his preoccupation with Rowan Hawes was eroded by the realization that all the windows were boarded up. He hammered on the door and tried to squint through the gaps between the boards.

'Looking for the Conchee?'

He turned to see an elderly couple wrapped up against the cold like a pair of Russians; they were dragging along an old black Labrador by a length of rope on a walk the animal was less than keen on completing. 'Mr Newsam, yes.'

'In prison,' the man replied. 'Refused to be conscripted. Got two years in Wormwood Scrubs. Hard Labour.'

'Nothing less than the coward deserved,' added his wife with a self-righteous toss of her scarfed head.

Her words spiked Max's ire as surely as the air pricking his cheeks. He hung his head at the thought of Newsam being so cruelly treated, being made to suffer so for his beliefs. How could a society respect a man for his ideals one minute and then revile him for them the next and still call itself humane and just? He felt his breath come in heavy gulps, and he blew his nose to clear it and his mind. His love had deserted him and now his confessor had been wrested from him. He was suddenly consumed with the worst of human emotions: he felt sorry for himself.

He drove to Littlemore through flurries of light snow, and stopped outside Zena's cottage trying to summon the courage to knock on her door. He'd not written since he went back to France, and her letters ceased after a couple of months. He pulled up the collar of his greatcoat and, against his first inclination, convinced himself he had all to gain and nothing to lose.

He decided to take no liberties and knocked on the front door like any normal visitor. It squeaked open an inch or two. He caught sight of Zena's beautiful face and his heart leapt.

'Max!' she said, gripping the edge of the door tightly. 'What are you doin' here?'

'I hoped I might wish you a Merry Christmas! May I come in?'

'I don't think that would be wise,' she replied, glancing over his shoulder.

'Why not? Have you someone in there?'

'Yes.'

'Don't you love me any more?'

'No, I don't.'

'You don't believe I love you, then?'

'No, I don't.'

'Can't I persuade you otherwise?'

'No, not no more.'

'Are you sure?'

'Max, I've given you plenty o' chances to prove it.'

'I can change if you'll give me the chance.'

Zena tapped her fingers on the door frame. 'My moind's made up. The answer's "No."'

'Can't I see you again?'

'No, I don't waunt to see you.'

'Isn't that harsh?'

'No.'

'Not after all these years?'

Zena had spent nights crying herself to sleep thinking of those years. She had come to terms with what she was. She was a whore. A beautiful one but still a whore. And men like Max Lanham were always going to treat her like a whore no matter what they said or promised her.

'Shouldn't you be with her?' she said, her voice spraying acid on the last word.

'Oh, so you know . . .'

'We all knows. Albert Bostock made sure o' that. An' I saw her comin' out o' Lawn Upton myself.'

'I understand . . .'

'Do you, Max?'

'Yes, I think I do.'

'When are you getting' married then?'

'That's not going to happen . . .'

'So, she's rejected you . . .'

'In a manner of speaking . . .'

'. . . an' you think you can come crawlin' back into my bed?'

'No, Zena, it's not like that at all!'

Her bottom lip bulged. 'I'm tired o' being used by men loik you. I thought you were better than that. I thought you wuz a proper man. But Hector wuz right! You've no iron in you. You're as weak as your father an' two-faced loik that ghastly woman you calls a mother!'

The door slammed shut and Max heard her crying. He retraced his steps to the car feeling lonelier than he had ever done, even lonelier than his terrified teenage self on the Black Bridge or during his recent ordeal at Caulaincourt.

He drove the car up the drive of Lawn Upton, taking stock of his life. He knew he was a murderer and believed he had betrayed a friend; he had disowned his parents and been abandoned by his one true love; now he had been denounced as a fake. He truly was an outcast.

He halted the Morris in front of the former coach-house latterly converted into a garage. He climbed out and pushed the doors. They barely yielded and a knocking noise came from the far side that resembled the hollow beat of a drum. Something was obstructing them. Max put his shoulder against the doors. They gave way and he tumbled inside to find himself staring at the soles of his father's brown Grenson boots.

Max looked up and saw the lifeless body of Roy Lanham twisting at the end of a rope secured to the heavy beam above the doors.

23

Holnon Wood Again

Max kept his room at the Tree Hotel, and in the weeks following Roy
Lanham's funeral he spent most days wandering the Thames backwaters,
keeping himself to himself. Cattle he could cope with; but not people.
He could scarcely cope with himself.

He had found Roy Lanham's diaries and scrapbooks on the morning
of the funeral when searching at the bottom of his father's shirt drawer
for a stiff white collar. The leather-bound scrapbooks were embossed
with titles in gold lettering: there was one for each of Max Lanham's
three seasons in the Magdalen College School First XV. The clippings
from the *Oxford Mail*, *Oxford Times* and the school magazine were
neatly stuck in and accompanied by his own comments: 'Marvellous
performance! Two tries! One with a jink and outside swerve any
international would be proud of! Certainly made me proud to watch!
Needs to speed up his pass, though! But I've great hopes of him!'

A paean of praise, page after page of eulogy. Why had he never
said anything? Max had rubbed his eyes, but still they surrendered
no tears: the chances waived, the missed opportunities. Chances and
opportunities now lost forever.

If the scrapbooks were a testament to a loving father the diaries
were evidence of a grieving husband. The names of his wife's lovers; his
desperation; his flight into the arms of the woman who served him the
alcohol he needed to escape; his desolation on being told by his wife

that she had aborted the second child he craved. And, above all, the feeling of self-loathing that burned through every entry once he had capitulated to his wife's blackmail.

'I am disgusted with myself. I cannot seem to function as a man, a husband or a father—God knows what young Max will think of me when he grows up and I cannot begin to think what will become of Flo and her boy,' he had written as long ago as 18 January 1903. 'I am utterly worn out. In mind and body; in soul and spirit.'

As Max chewed on that entry his love of words diminished. And he started to wonder whether there was any point in him carrying on. Each day he paused beneath the Black Bridge, imagining what it would feel like to jump into the water with pockets weighed down with stones, begging the water to end his suffering. Would he embrace death like a man or would he struggle for life like a coward? Could he fall on his sword like Mark Antony or would he be like Brutus and need help

Clambering up the embankment, he walked to the centre arch and stared down into the black water which seemed to him as if it were holding up a mirror to his soul. His brain began to swirl along with the currents, and after a few minutes he climbed down again and sat beneath the bridge, banging his fists into his temples. He was more like Brutus than he cared to admit.

In March he received a letter from his mother in which she professed her deep love for him and her desire for some kind of *rapprochement*. Max re-read it to check he had not missed anything; but there was still no evidence of a guilty conscience, no hint of a remorse. Max smiled ruefully: at least she was consistent. She would find another sap and cultivate a surrogate son.

The communication had been triggered, Naomi Lanham insisted, by the arrival at Lawn Upton of a letter addressed to him from Canada. The envelope was postmarked Toronto; it carried no return address. Max ripped it open in the faint hope that its contents were an invitation to join Rowan Hawes at the earliest opportunity, or even the news that she was returning to England to be with him. His hands shook when he read the opening paragraph explaining how the letter was the outcome of her having a vivid dream about him which left her alarmed for his safety. But his hopes were as quickly dashed. She had no intention of returning. She was about to embark on a trans-continental train journey that would enable her to see Canada and bring her to

Vancouver, where she intended forging a new life for herself. There was no suggestion of him having any place in that life.

She had taken days and many crumpled drafts to compose the letter. Each passing week had seen her reconsidering whether her instant departure was a gesture too grand, but as Max had not responded to the letter she'd left with Mrs Beenham—which she was sure he would—he must have treated it as conclusive.

Max's revelations had shattered her belief in him and, she thought, her inviolable love for him. Perhaps her feelings toward him were mere affection not love, for love, she had told herself, conquers all. Now she was less convinced. Perhaps he deserved a second chance. Should a man's future be dictated by one moment of weakness? Should donning a hair shirt burden him forever? She tried in vain to write those words but a combination of uncertainty and stubbornness prevented her. She ended by saying she would write again when she was settled. But as she stuck the stamp on the envelope she knew in her heart that she wanted him to follow her. If he loved her, if they loved each other and were meant for each other, he would come.

Max read and re-read her letter until the paper became frayed. He resolved that if he got out of this war alive he would take ship to Canada and trawl every street and every house in Vancouver until he found her.

Toward the end of the month Max was reclassified A1 and returned to active duty. The high command was concerned at the relative absence of German activity: it believed the enemy were preparing for a major offensive, in which case experienced officers like Max were invaluable assets. Max was less concerned with its motive. All he cared about was its decision. He had lost his father and disowned his mother. But he did have a brother. And he was somewhere in France.

Any immediate hopes of finding Chick were scuppered by the Germans. On the morning of 21 March a tremendous bombardment preceded a concerted attack through the dense morning fog along the entire Western Front from Ypres in the north to Rheims in the south. The British were outnumbered four to one, and its 'Battle' line around St Quentin was annihilated and smashed back 30 miles toward Amiens: it was the greatest gain by either side since 1914. Max rejoined the remnants of the Oxfords in Marcelcave following an abortive counter-attack on 27 March. It was his 23rd birthday.

The Battalion was glad to see him. It had moved south to Arras from the Ypres sector shortly after the failed attack on Hill 35, and from there back to the Somme to spend a freezing Christmas near Bray before settling at its former stamping ground of Holnon Wood, where it guarded the Fayet-Gricourt section of the front line. It had borne the brunt of the German offensive. Only one officer returned unscathed from the front trenches; all four company commanders were dead or missing—including Adamson, shot through the head. The news of 16 platoon was equally grim: Clinkard was reported missing and that those who could be accounted for alive numbered barely a dozen. Max enquired of the adjutant whether any private by the name of Collicutt had arrived in the March batch of replacements; he checked the list and replied in the negative.

Max trudged down the main road to Amiens, passing a rag-taggle caravan comprising men from any number of different units. There was no panic, no hurry, no shouting or yelling, just a dogged steady slog towards safety. Some men were carrying hens under their arms or bottles of wine, one held an open one to his lips. The few officers did nothing. This was a rabble not an army.

Max reached a collection of tents he was told held most of the Oxfords and searched through them for any of his old men. He found the debris of defeat and withdrawal everywhere: broken bodies, broken spirits; the sobs and wails of wounded men on all sides; and the occasional shriek of despair. Filth and ruin stretched in every direction: helmets, haversacks and gas masks, their owners dead or fled; Lewis guns and a tri-podded Vickers machine gun amid a nest of shells, rifles impaled on their bayonets; trucks and field guns lying abandoned on their sides like so many beached whales; and packets of unopened shirts and socks where once a quartermaster's stores had been. This was the landscape of defeat, thought Max as he surveyed it. As wholesale a defeat as he had ever witnessed. The war was on the brink of being lost.

Eventually he came across Pitson sitting on a tree stump, a soiled bandage round his forehead, a smoking cigarette dangling from his lips. Pitson did not recognize his former officer: he continued blowing pillars of smoke into the air and staring at something only he could see in the distance.

'Pitson, it's me, Lt Lanham.'

'Is it?' mumbled Pitson, squinting at him through the cigarette smoke. 'Saw Gibbo cop one in the guts. Pulker too. Standin' roight next to me, he were. Christ, how the bugger screamed! There's only me an' Summers from the old mob, sir. The gang's pretty much all gone now . . .'

Max patted him on the back, and sent him off to the MO to get himself a ticket for the base hospital. Pitson hobbled a few steps using his rifle as a crutch before halting . . .

'Mister Lanham,' he called. 'here's one for yer! Guess who I bumped into at a boxing show in Ugny? Only that young pal o' yours, Chick whatever his name is.'

Max ran toward him. 'Are you positive? He's not on the roll . . .'

'Wouldn't be, would he . . .'

'What do you mean? Explain yourself man?'

'He were with the Berks, were'n he!'

'Damn it!'

The Berks had been held in reserve until thrown into the Battle Line at Maissemy as part of a desperate counter-attacking manoeuvre and had also suffered horrendous casualties, including their commanding officer killed while leading his men on horseback. Details of their survivors proved as sketchy as those of the Oxfords, but Max eventually found Chick's platoon sergeant.

'I hope the little bastard copped it!' he told Max. 'Last I saw of him he was running away towards bloody Amiens like a fuckin' jack rabbit with a greyhound on its arse! If I see him again I'll shoot him me-bloody-self!'

Max did not doubt the sergeant's threat. In any event, Chick may have been killed during this wholesale retreat, and no one would be any the wiser. He had done all he could and needed sleep. He would resume his quest in the morning. The following day proved no more informative, and it became increasingly tricky for him to avoid the urgent duties associated with the Oxfords' withdrawal to the west of Amiens without drawing attention to himself.

He was up with the light on the morning of the 29th. It was a clear, sharp dawn, the kind of morning that would propel him from his bed at Lawn Upton and send him dashing down to Sandford or Iffley with rod in hand eager to get at the perch and the pike and the roach. As he contemplated escaping the bedlam around him he realized he would not be the only person whose mind would be so inclined. If, that is, the person in question was still alive. He stopped a passing medical orderly and asked him if there was a stream or river within walking distance.

Had there been a lock Max could have been back at Iffley and not outside a French village called Cachy. Nor was there Rowan Hawes beside him to put a smile on his face. He should be searching for her, he thought, not his half-brother. She could be waiting somewhere for him to materialize as he had that evening in Biggleswade. She could be sat somewhere alone: reading Byron and Yeats, pining for his touch and his intellect; trying to busy herself with needle and thread—but longing for him to rescue her from such dreariness.

But there was no rattle of the lock-keeper's key nor giggle from the throat of Rowan Hawes. Not a human sound disturbed the pastoral dawn overture of running water and birds singing in the willows as the rising sun played tricks with the ripples.

Max would recognize Chick anywhere, but on a riverbank it was too easy: with a rod in his long arms he looked like a dockside crane hanging over the water. Max watched him bait and cast his line into midstream and stole up behind him.

'Are they biting, Chick?' he said quietly.

'A few, Master Max. Just a few. Sneaky beggars they are. Usin' the current to get past me.'

Chick shook his head, continuing to play out more line to the red-tipped float being carried downstream.

'Why not take a rest now? I've a bit of bread and cheese here . . .'

'Ma's san-widges?'

'Almost as good.'

Chick lay down his rod and turned. The look on his face also turned, from glazed to shocked as if disconnection from the fishing rod had reconnected him with reality.

'Master Max, what are you doin' here?'

'Looking for you, Chick, what else?'

It was then Max registered that Chick was dressed in the ill-fitting apparel of a French peasant.

'Where's your uniform?' he said, grabbing Chick's sleeve.

Chick's eyes examined the cloth closely. 'Dunno.'

Max shook him violently. 'You blessed fool! If you're found like this you're as good as dead! Don't you realize that?'

Max looked over each shoulder and then dragged Chick under the nearest willow. 'Where's your uniform? You must get back into it!'

'I loik these clothes better . . .'

'For Christ's sake snap out of it!'

'. . . found 'em on a washin' line.'

Max slapped him hard. Chick waded into the water up to his knees. He scooped up a handful of pebbles and started snivelling.

'What's possessed you

Chick ignored him and began skimming the stones he'd collected. He bent his body parallel to the surface and a whip-cracked them across the water in rapid succession.

'Look at that! Every bugger's sunk! Not one bounce! I got a tenner last summer. Stones no good, see. Not flat enough. Wastin' me time with pebbly ones . . .'

His head sagged, and the more he snivelled the more his body crumpled and reality seized control of his addled senses. He sank into the water just as Max's arms grabbed him.

Max dragged him onto the bank and wiped his face dry. Chick looked younger than ever: truly, thought Max, a fish out of water. Chick began mumbling, at first barely audibly.

'I just walked in the recruitin' office. "How old are you, me lad?" the doc said. I looked him straight in the eye an' said, "17 ½, sir," an' he said, "Run along an' come back when you're nineteen . . . tomorra." So thass what I done. Only I reckoned I'd better play safe. So I went to Reading an' enlisted there. The sarge looked me up an' down an' went "Hmmm, what does your mum think of you goin' for a sol-jer?" I told him she wuz dyin'. He just patted me on the shoulder, an' signed me acceptance without 'nother word.'

Max sat down beside him and gave him a hug. 'Chick, you poor, silly, boy. Why couldn't you just be patient . . .'

Max heard the crack of twigs snapping under the weight of boots, and looked up to see two Redcaps.

'We'll take things from here.'

'Thank you for leading us to him, lieutenant,' added the other.

Max released his grip on Chick as the first Redcap lifted him upright. 'Come on lad. Don't be giving us any trouble.'

Max watched Chick rub his eyes, and he heard himself saying 'This boy wouldn't hurt a . . .' But he couldn't finish the sentence.

24

Chateau Bagatelle

Chick's FGCM was convened on 5 April at Chateau Bagatelle, well to the rear of the fighting lines, near Abbeville. The court comprised a senior officer acting as President, a Major Brough from the 2/5th Gloucesters who had fought alongside the Royal Berkshire Regiment in the recent attack, plus two officers from the Berks, a captain and a subaltern with his arm in a sling who looked even younger than Chick.

Max entered the court-room—an airy high-ceilinged salon full of light pouring through a pair of magnificent Neo-classical windows but freezing cold as a result—alongside his legal adversary, the adjutant from the Berks.

'Ratcliffe, prosecuting officer.'

'Lanham, "Prisoner's Friend", defending,' Max replied shaking the proffered hand.

'This is cut and dried, you realize. You really needn't bother.'

Max glared at him. 'A kangaroo court, you mean?'

'Certainly not. A legal eagle from the Judge Advocate's Branch is in attendance to advise on procedures and ensure everything is above board.'

'In that case, we'll see, shall we?'

Ratcliffe shot him a condescending smile and, taking their seats at separate tables, they waited for the three panel members to enter.

The panel sat down behind a longer table, directly in front of which was a wooden chair. It might have been a dress rehearsal for Chick's firing squad, thought Max. Chick was marched in, hatless and beltless, and stood at attention as the court orderly read out the charge: 'The accused, Private 306453 C Collicutt, when on active service did desert His Majesty's Service in that at Ugny on 21 March 1918 he absented himself from the front lines and then again on 24 March until apprehended in civilian clothing at Cachy on 29 March 1918.'

'How do you plead?' asked the President.

Chick looked toward Max, who smiled and nodded. 'Not guilty,' said Chick firmly and looking straight ahead, as Max had coached him.

'I couldn't hear that clearly,' boomed the President.

'Not guilty, sir,' Chick repeated, more nervously.

The President wrote down Chick's plea. 'Now, let's get on.'

'Desertion during active service is one of the most serious crimes a soldier can commit,' began Ratcliffe, 'and I shall prove to the Court without any doubt that the accused is guilty of precisely that offence.'

He called the first witness, Chick's platoon sergeant, Stratton, who proceeded under oath to repeat, in less colourful language, what he had told Max.

'We were in reserve at Ugny on the mornin' of the 21st and I saw the accused runnin' away as soon as the bombardment commenced. He went to pieces, practically off his head in sheer terror. He was a positive danger to anyone around him, making them as terrified as he was. I told him to stop or I'd shoot. But he ignored me an' kept on runnin'. I did not see him again until the 24th when we were at Verlaines fightin' a rearguard action. I asked him where he'd been. He said nothin', an' when the Boche attack began on the 25th I saw him runnin' away again. I shouted at him but he kept on goin'.'

Max rose to cross-examine, and was told to sit down by the President: 'The facts are indisputable. The accused wouldn't be on a charge if the facts weren't correct. Don't let the court's time be wasted.'

'But it's possible that Private Collicutt was merely absent without leave on the first occasion and totally disorientated by the time of the subsequent attack . . .'

'Possible, but extremely unlikely in my opinion,' sneered the President out of the corner of his mouth to his co-judges. 'Shall we move on?'

The next witness sworn was one of the Redcaps who confirmed Chick was wearing civilian clothes when apprehended at Cachy. Max gestured to the President that the evidence given was not in dispute.

The only other witness called by the prosecution was the Regimental Medical Officer who declared that he had examined Private Collicutt on 30 March and found him to be perfectly sane.

'Therefore responsible for his actions?' emphasized the President.

'Yes, quite so,' the RMO confirmed.

'Then you may stand down.'

Again Max rose. 'Just a few questions to the RMO if you please.'

The President looked as if he just felt bird droppings fall on his head. 'Very well!'

Max turned to the RMO, a man whose gaunt appearance advertised the tasks lately required of him.

'Had you any previous occasion to examine Private Collicutt?'

'He came to me on the 14th, the 15th and the 20th of March.'

'For what reason?'

'He said he was feeling sick, in his stomach.' He looked toward the panel. 'He had the tom-tits.'

The witness's shoulders sagged as he finished the sentence.

'And?'

The RMO sighed. 'He looked pale, drawn. But then most men are. His vital signs were satisfactory, and I found him to be suffering from no appreciable disease and marked him "duty". I told him it was just tiredness, or some dodgy tin of bully, and that he was perfectly fit for duty in the trenches.'

'Physically fit, yes. But what about his mental state? Did you notice anything untoward?'

'He was dull, morose, seemed rather nervous.'

'In what way?' asked Max, suddenly leaning forward onto his knuckles. 'How did he display this nervousness?'

The RMO looked up to the ceiling for a few seconds before answering. 'He kept raising his feet alternately off the ground and jerking his head from side to side.'

'Are such tics usually found in a stable personality? Do you see it often?

'No, in the first instance. Yes, in the second instance—but often it's put on for my benefit so the man can be written up as unfit for duty.'

'And in Private Collicutt's case?'

'Given his youth, and his callowness, I suppose one could say he was under some genuine pressure.'

Max straightened. 'So, in your expert medical opinion, the accused was under extreme pressure?'

'I'm no expert on mental health, you understand, and I made no examination of him to ascertain his mental condition. But, yes, I'd say so.'

'And when was that?'

'On the 20th, the last time I saw him.'

'In other words,' Max intoned exultantly, 'the day before the German bombardment and offensive began?'

Max thanked him, and Ratcliffe rose to re-direct.

'Do you see lots of men exhibiting the accused's alleged symptoms?'

'Yes.'

'Do they all run away under fire?'

.No, not to my knowledge. Nearly all of them do their duty.'

'Thank you,' Ratcliffe said, followed by a sideways glance toward Max and then another toward the panel. 'Sir, that concludes the case for the prosecution.'

'Mister Lanham, do you have anything to say in the accused's defence?' said the President briskly.

'Yes, there is much I wish to place before this court on Private Collicutt's behalf.'

'Do you have any witnesses to contradict the evidence we've already heard?'

'Not exactly, sir, but . . .'

'But what?'

'I believe there are certain factors that should first be accepted in mitigation.'

'Do you now,' said the President, looking toward the advisor from JAB.

'Mitigating circumstances may be raised after the verdict has been decided,' the advocate announced. 'Before sentencing.'

'But . . .'

'No buts, Mister Lanham. Your next point, please.'

Max shuffled his papers and breathed deeply in an effort to hold his temper.

'There was no premeditation here, only extreme provocation . . .'

The advocate again exchanged nods with the President. 'Later, Mister Lanham, if you please. Once again, this falls into the category of extenuating circumstances. Do you have any witnesses for the defence?'

'I'd like to call the Brigade Medical Officer . . .'

'Another medic?' boomed the President. 'We've had one!'

'The accused was examined after his apprehension, sir, and the findings were significant.'

'Oh, very well.'

The BMO was sworn in and testified that he examined the prisoner at Cachy on the evening of the 29th shortly after his arrest, with particular attention being paid to his mental health.

The BMO lifted his chin and summed up: 'I found Private Collicutt to be below average intelligence and although not of unsound mind, he was suffering from a marked degree of neurasthenia . . .'

'Which means?' interrupted Max.

'Mental disability.'

'Shell shock?'

'Some call it that, yes.'

Ratcliffe sprang to his feet to cross examine the witness. 'Only one question. Could you say for certain whether Private Collicutt's mental state preceded or resulted from the actions between 21st and 25th March?'

'No way of telling, I'm afraid.'

The panel exchanged glances, and the President took a couple of minutes to record his version of what he had just heard.

'Any further witnesses, Mister Lanham?' he said eventually.

'Only Private Collicutt.'

'Then let him give his evidence on oath.'

Chick gripped the arms of his chair and rose unsteadily to his feet. He placed a hand on the bible and read out the oath just as unsteadily.

'Private Collicutt,' said Max, 'tell the court in your own words what happened on the 21st March.'

'Well, sir, I'd bin feelin' giddy for days. All that rain, rain, rain. Mud an' the slush. Always wet uniform an' cold pants an' socks. Nothin' ever dry. No proper shelter. Hopeless food. Vomitin' an' nothin' but the trots every blessed day. The carryin' parties, the workin' parties, the drillin', the snipin', the shellin'. Makes you waunner die . . . .'

Chick began rubbing his eyes.

'Try to continue,' Max encouraged, 'in your own time . . .'

'I'd bin to see the doc an' he told me to carry on best I could. Then the big shellin' started up, an' I got real dizzy. I dunno what I wuz doin'. I wuz walkin' up an' down the communications trench when I think the sarge must have shouted at me. The noise wuz makin' me head hurt so bad I just started runnin' away from it, I s'pose . . .'

Chick began to mumble inaudibly into his chest.

'Do you remember anything else?' Max prompted.

'No, not really . . .'

'Where did you go?'

'Dunno . . .'

'Do you remember rejoining your unit a few days later?'

'No.'

'Do you recall putting on civilian clothes?'

'I went down to this farm . . . I thought I wuz dressed funny . . . an' I tried to find me proper clobber . . . but you found me a'fore I could.'

Max tried to conceal a wince at Chick's unconvincing answer to his final question: why couldn't the stupid boy have just said he remembered nothing.

Chick's eyebrows and lips began working at odds with each other. 'But iss all jus' a blur.'

Max smiled and sat down. Ratcliffe got to his feet.

'So, Private Collicutt, you remember nothing until Mister Lanham found you by the river at Cachy? You don't recall Sergeant Stratton ordering you to stop running away, on not one occasion but two? And, most importantly of all, you do not recall somehow obtaining civilian clothes and deliberately, I repeat, deliberately changing into them with the intention of deceiving?'

Chick slowly shook his head. The significance of Ratcliffe's last assertion was not lost on Max or the panel and the prosecutor resumed his seat with a smug look on his face.

'Is that all, Mister Lanham?' said the President. 'If so, it is my duty to thank you for your eloquence, which the Court will take into its deliberations. The Court will now retire to consider its verdict in private.'

The court rose as the panel departed.

'This shouldn't take long,' said Ratcliffe, offering Max a cigarette.

Max sensed he was right but was not about to give him that satisfaction. 'I wouldn't be so sure if I were you.'

'Don't be so obtuse!' replied Ratcliffe, face flushed. 'We're losing 400 men every day! We're on the run. I'm sorry to say this but the Battalion is demoralized. Morale is rock bottom. Too many degenerates are being sent over nowadays. Ten men in a thousand are deserting. That's 10,000 men in an army of one million, two whole brigades! Examples must be made. What's one more man?'

The door to the ante-room opened and the three officers of the panel returned to their seats. Barely four minutes had elapsed since their departure.

'The prisoner will stand!'

The President tried to look the accused directly in the eye but Chick stared resolutely at the floor.

'The Court has a bounden duty to assume that the accused intended the natural and probable consequences of his actions. It has considered the circumstances in which he absented himself and the length of time during which he remained absent, and the probability of that absence leading to the avoidance of dangerous duties. The court finds the prisoner guilty as charged and sentences him to suffer death by being shot.'

Max looked down at his papers and closed his eyes.

'I'm gunner be shot?' Chick blabbed, prompting the escorts to restrain him.

'Now you may plead your mitigating circumstances, Mister Lanham,' said the President.

Max stood, with little conviction in body or voice. 'In the first place, there is the question of the prisoner's age . . .'

The President held up a sheet of paper and waved it at Max. 'States here on his B122 he was aged 19 when he enlisted on 2 December 1917.'

'That is incorrect, sir. He was only just past his 17th birthday. In fact he should either have been sent home or else classified A4 and sent to a Young Soldiers Battalion well to the rear of the firing line instead of being asked to fight after just 14 weeks basic training.'

'Says here he is 19,' repeated the President, neither his thick countryman's fingers nor his patrician tones betraying any sign of tension. 'If it's on the form he signed in December that is his official age as far as the Army is concerned. In any event the prisoner's youth is no excuse.'

Max dug his fingernails into the table.

'Anything more?' asked the President.

'There is the issue of provocation taking precedence over premeditation in this instance. This is surely an important distinction for the Court to recognize. Had it been the other way round the case against Private Collicutt would have been damning indeed. His actions were not premeditated, he did not plan to desert.'

Max pointed to Chick. 'Look at him. He could not plan a day's fishing. I have known the prisoner all his life and I can assure you he is incapable of reasoning, planning and carrying out anything!'

Max felt his chest throb and his voice wobble.

'He was no shirker. He was merely fragile. He had volunteered to fight for his country at the dictates of his own young heart. He failed. And for that failure he has been brought here to plead for his life.'

'But Mister Lanham,' the JAB officer interjected, 'the intention to desert is quite clear in this case. The accused was found in civilian clothes. It is abundantly clear that he had no intention, and therefore no plan, to rejoin his unit. Premeditation is self-evident. This was not a matter of going AWOL. The prisoner's actions betrayed a calculating regard for his own personal safety. It was a cold blooded and deliberate crime of the meanest description.'

'It was an act borne of fear!' Max insisted loudly. 'And we all—even yourself and the President—have known fear.'

The President's jaw jutted like a battleship's ram.

'But we all react in a different way. Some of us feel fear but do not show it. Some of us feel fear and show it but somehow manage to do our jobs.'

Max paused and looked down at Chick, wondering what was going through his young unformed mind as he listened to arguments he could not understand from men with the power to decide whether he should live or die.

'And then there are men like Private Collicutt,' Max continued solemnly, 'who feel fear, show it and cannot carry out their duties.

We cannot, and should not, just take the easy option and shoot them all.'

The President fiddled with his papers, making some sort of reference to the argument Max had mounted, and then cleared his throat as aggressively as any man of authority might when that authority has been impugned by a junior officer whom he considered an upstart.

'Then I shall draw these proceedings to a close.'

'Is that it?' jabbered Chick. 'Am I gunner be shot?'

'Calm down, Chick,' Max muttered in his ear. 'Sentence has to be confirmed. There's still a chance. It must go in front of the Brigade commander and then the Judge Advocate General's team at GHQ before going to General Haig. He's the only man with the legal power to confirm a death sentence.'

Chick was led away and taken back under escort to Bovelles where the Berks were in rest and lodged in the *estaminet* pressed into service as a guard room. A week later he had just finished playing cards with Max when a captain entered to read out the news he was having nightmares about. There was to be no commutation of sentence. He was to die.

Ratcliffe had been correct: no one in the chain of command had spoken up for Chick. Max was given access to the papers and read for himself the damning verdict of Chick's commanding officer: 'I've no personal knowledge of this man but I'm of the opinion he was so frightened of shell fire that he deliberately preferred to take his chance of the consequences rather than remain under it. I am of the opinion the man is not worth keeping. For the sake of example the extreme penalty should be inflicted.' Underneath the Brigadier-General had added: 'This man is a degenerate, quite worthless, with no intention of fighting for his country. He is better removed from this world.' And scrawled across the bottom in red ink was Haig's confirmation of sentence and the bleak postscript: 'How can we ever win if this plea is allowed?'

The death sentence was promulgated before the Berks that evening, execution of sentence to be put into effect the following morning. Chick was in a state of virtual collapse and had to be supported to and from the parade.

Max returned to the *estaminet* with him and told him he would be back after supper to sit with him through the night.

Chick fell to the floor and curled up like a baby.

'Don't tell me mum!' he sobbed. 'Please don't tell me mum!'

25

Bovelles

Max ran his tongue along the gum to seal the envelope and then propped it against the pocket edition of *A Tale of Two Cities* he'd been reading, along with the other two letters he'd just written. One was to Chick's mother; one was to Zena; and the last was addressed to Rowan Hawes, care of her mother in Biggleswade. None had been easy to compose in spite of their brevity. He had no words for his mother; his efforts lay balled on the floor.

Max got up and buckled on his Sam Browne. He picked up the revolver from the table and spun the chamber to check its contents. Taking one last look round the room, he put on his cap and made to leave, but spotting the ball of paper he took measured aim and kicked it to the back of the grate. He smiled with content at his skill and then watched the flames do their job just as effectively. She was gone from his life at last and he felt all the freer for it.

He reached for the door handle. Then stopped. He shut the door, returned to the table and picked up the envelope addressed to Rowan Hawes. He ripped it open and extracted the letter. Removing his cap, he extricated the gold chain from beneath his collar and lifted it over his head. He kissed the St Jude medal before wrapping it inside the letter, which he inserted into a fresh envelope and re-addressed. Then he was prepared to leave the room.

Max knocked on the guard-room door and was admitted by the sergeant of the guard. The hovel, for that's all it could be described as, reeked of wet grass clippings, courtesy of its usual occupation as the gardener's shed, and from the thick fumes of two oil lamps that provided some dim artificial light to augment the natural light entering from one smallish window set high on the wall. Stood against the remaining three walls of the cell, which measured about a dozen yards square, were guards with shouldered arms: Chick's cot, were he able to entertain sleep, occupied one corner. The only other item of furniture was a table positioned below the window at which the padre sat opposite the condemned man, trying to engage him in conversation.

Chick was hunched over the table, elbows crooked and head in hands, a half-filled glass in front of him. He looked up as Max entered and tried to smile but the smile merely collapsed into a grimace.

'Fancy a drink o' rum?' he said, trying to cobble a manly expression together.

Max asked the padre to move and, taking the chair, smiled weakly at Chick as if he were doing no more than bringing grapes to a sick friend.

'Don't mind if I do!' he replied cheerfully.

Chick poured him a healthy tot, they clinked glasses and emptied them in one swallow. The rum burnt Max's throat and made him shake his head. He glanced at the bottle and saw it was already half empty. Chick refilled the glasses and downed his with the alacrity of a desert explorer stumbling across an oasis.

'I waunts you to take this,' he said, reaching inside his tunic. 'Iss only me paybook. I've filled in the Sol-jer's Will bit at the back, loik they tell us.'

Max took the AB64 and read the page Chick had left open: 'If I get killed all I have to come from the government for my services I leave to Mrs F Collicutt, George Inn, Littlemore.'

Max felt like bursting into tears. He had no idea what to say or how to react. All he knew was that on no account must he burst into tears. He handed the paper back to Chick and nodded.

'Are you bearing-up, Chick?' he said, playing with his glass in an effort to suppress the lightheadedness that was threatening to shut down his thought processes.

'I don't loik this waitin'. Thought I wuz frightened on the Black Bridge but . . .'

Max pursed his lips, grateful that the opportunity he wanted had presented itself so soon.

'And you were frightened? Really petrified by the time you got up top?'

'Yeh. Wuzn't you?'

'Looking down at that black swirling water? Wondering what it would feel like to drop 20 feet and how the impact would sting every square inch of your whole body until it throbbed?'

'Too bloody roight I wuz! Thought I wuz sure to shit me pants. If I'd stood there much longer I would've had shit all over me legs! I had to come down . . .'

Chick thoughts wrinkled his brow for a moment. 'Thass why I knows I'm not brave enough for this.'

'You were brave then and you will be tomorrow.'

Chick's mouth ceased twitching. 'Whad'ya mean?'

'You see, Chick, when a man gets so afraid he thinks he can't manage, that fear turns back on itself and becomes instead a strange brand of courage. It's like hot and cold. When something gets really cold it can burn like any fire. Cold becomes hot.'

'Yeh, I get it! Like rollin' a snowball! So bloody cold, if you keeps it in your hand too long it starts to burn loik blazes!'

Max nodded. 'In the same way, fear can turn into courage. That's why you came down. Because out of your fear you manufactured the courage to do what you knew was right for you, for yourself. And that's why you'll get through this ordeal as well.'

Max examined Chick's eyes for signs of understanding but they remained blank and blinking.

'Easy for you to say, Master Max,' mumbled Chick. 'You're one o' the bravest men I've ever known . . .'

'Do you think so?'

'I do! I seen you jump the Black Bridge! An' you're a war 'ero, an' all!'

Max interlocked his fingers, placed his hands on the table and looked Chick directly in the eyes.

'Well, let me tell you something. You don't need to be courageous to jump off that bridge. I jumped and there was nothing brave about it.'

Chick's mouth fell open, and he jack-knifed in his chair as if a pole had been thrust down the back of his shirt. 'Don't be bloody stupid!'

'I jumped because I didn't have the courage to refuse. You did. You had the courage to come down and live with the consequences. I didn't. And you'll summon the courage to get through this tomorrow.'

'You're havin' me on?'

'No, I'm not. Honest to God.'

'You jumped cuz you wuz too scared not to?'

'Yes.'

'I dunno . . .'said Chick, shaking his head. 'Can't reck'n that!'

Max knew that if he was going to say what he wanted to say it would have to be now. He hoped his words would help not hinder Chick's situation. But, were he honest, he wanted to say them for his own peace of mind, for his own satisfaction.

'And there's one other reason I know you have the courage to get through this,' he said, raising his voice slightly to gain Chick's full attention. 'We've known each other a long time, haven't we?'

'I s'pose.'

'Been like brothers, haven't we?'

'Yes.'

'Understood each other?'

'Yes.'

'Could've been brothers . . .'

'Huh!' Chick snorted 'Apart from me bein' nothin' but a yokel an' you bein' a gent!'

Max hesitated. 'What if I were to tell you that we are brothers?'

Chick rocked his chair back and forth. 'Get away! Stop foolin' about!'

He stopped rocking, and began beating on the table like an over wound toy drummer.

Max grabbed his wrists. 'Just listen to me, Chick.'

'This better be good!'

'At Christmas I discovered . . .'

'How wuz that then?' Chick laughed. 'In a cracker?'

'No matter. I discovered that my father is also your father . . .'

'Bullshit!'

'It's the truth. However unlikely it may seem. It surprised me as much as it surprises you. But it doesn't alter the fact that it's true.'

'I think you need 'nother drink!'

'Chick, you and I are half brothers.'

Chick looked into Max's eyes, and he stopped pouring. 'You're serious, en't you?'

Max squeezed Chick's hands, and nodded.

Chick's face lit up, the redness brought out by the rum varnished to a shiny crimson 'Well I never! Mister Lanham's me dad? The horny ol' goat!'

'Yes, he is.'

'How is he then?' piped Chick, adopting his version of a posh voice. 'Our dad?'

Max watched Chick grin, but ignored his enquiry.

'Sounds good, dunnit? Dad!'

'And it's because of that,' Max continued, 'because we have a common bond, that I know you'll get through this.'

Chick started to cry. 'No, I know I'll disgrace meself! Look at me now!'

His hands went below the table top and clutched his groin. 'I can feel meself Peein' meself now! An' they en't even tied me to the blinkin' chair yet!'

Max pictured himself on the Black Bridge, and reminded himself that this time there could be no shirking. He visualized the book left on his table open at its last page and heard the words of Sydney Carton: 'It is a far, far better thing I do, than I have ever done.'

He swallowed some more rum and with it his fear. He knew now more than ever what had to be done. What he must do. The responsibility he must take. He had seen a broken young boy reduced to a wretched specimen of humanity once, and was not going to stand by and watch it happen again. Not when the boy was his brother.

Max watched death and dawn creeping beneath the door, hand in hand like Cain and Abel. 'Come here, brother,' he said softly as he stood up from the table. 'Come and give your brother a hug.'

Max held out his arms and welcomed his brother into his embrace, subtly positioning him so that Chick obscured him from the guards. The feel of Chick's trembling body banished his own shakes, and with them any fears concerning the rectitude of what he was about to do. His right hand slipped down to his holster, and as he kissed Chick on the cheek he removed the Webley.

'Look at those stars up there,' he said. 'One for each of us. See that group over there? That's Gemini. The twins.'

Chick looked up at the heavens and began to laugh. 'Can't see me mum being your mum! Don't be daft!'

'That's you and there's me. Don't you see?'

'Wish mother'd told me . . .'

'You can forgive her keeping it to herself . . .'

'I dunno.'

'They say that when you forgive, you love,' said Max quietly. 'And when you love God shines a light on you.'

Chick's face broke into a quivering smile as the first rays of dawn broke through the shuttered windows and streaked his face.

'There, told you,' said Max.

The smile was still on Chick's face as Max gently positioned the revolver against his chest and pulled the trigger. His father had always told him that when a faithful old hunter has to be put down, always do it to the sound of the bugled tally-ho so it can leave the world on a happy note.

Max heard the muffled bang, smelt the singed fabric and felt his brother's body recoil, and then transfer its weight into his own arms. He felt the warmth of Chick's blood on his jacket, glueing them together in death as they'd never been bonded in life.

Max held him tight and sniffed away a tear. 'Stay strong. Sleep tight.'

ALL THE HEAVY DAYS ARE OVER
WB Yeats

They came for him as soon as the first rays of sunlight began to brighten the patchy remnants of the once extensive lawns at the rear of the chateau.

'It is a far, far better rest that I go to, than I have ever known,' he recited to himself as they marched him across to the chair placed against a wall of sand-bags. Yet to him it was no execution chair they bound him to. It was a mercy seat.

He watched the robin flutter away on an up-draught, and wondered if Rowan Hawes would ever spy a bird ascending one day and think of him flying free as he was now imagining her.

While they completed the preparations to put him to death in the manner prescribed by military law. he steadied himself by thinking only of her and was crying out to her in his heart when the bullets ripped open his chest. His fingers uncurled and the twisted envelope fell to the ground, the strands of her hair drifting away on the breeze.

Max Lanham's troubles were finally at an end; the burden of the Black Bridge finally cast off. His spirit had found peace; his soul was at rest.

Lightning Source UK Ltd.
Milton Keynes UK
UKOW041959301112

203004UK00002B/51/P